When in doubt, follow the trail.

Two-print Track Pattern — Walk, Trot, Bound

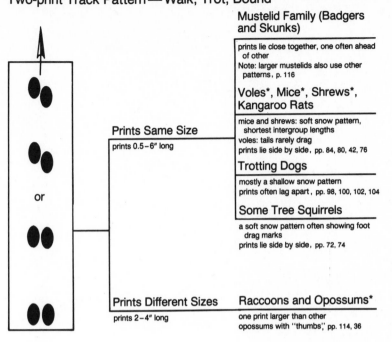

Mustelid Family (Badgers and Skunks)

prints lie close together, one often ahead of other
Note: larger mustelids also use other patterns, p. 116

Voles*, Mice*, Shrews*, Kangaroo Rats

mice and shrews: soft snow pattern, shortest intergroup lengths
voles: tails rarely drag
prints lie side by side, pp. 84, 80, 42, 76

Trotting Dogs

mostly a shallow snow pattern
prints often lag apart, pp. 98, 100, 102, 104

Some Tree Squirrels

a soft snow pattern often showing foot drag marks
prints lie side by side, pp. 72, 74

Prints Same Size
prints 0.5–6" long

Prints Different Sizes
prints 2–4" long

Raccoons and Opossums*

one print larger than other
opossums with "thumbs", pp. 114, 36

or

Four-print Track Pattern — Jump (Hop, Bound)
Larger hind feet usually fall ahead of front-foot prints

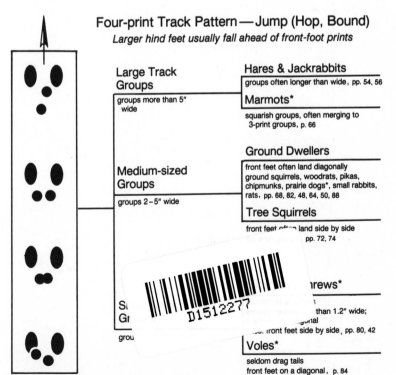

Large Track Groups
groups more than 5" wide

Hares & Jackrabbits
groups often longer than wide, pp. 54, 56

Marmots*
squarish groups, often merging to 3-print groups, p. 66

Medium-sized Groups
groups 2–5" wide

Ground Dwellers
front feet often land diagonally
ground squirrels, woodrats, pikas, chipmunks, prairie dogs*, small rabbits, rats, pp. 68, 82, 48, 64, 50, 88

Tree Squirrels
front feet often land side by side
pp. 72, 74

...rews*
...than 1.2" wide;
...front feet side by side, pp. 80, 42

Voles*
seldom drag tails
front feet on a diagonal, p. 84

Animals with variable gaits. Expect other track patterns.

Field Guide to Tracking Animals in Snow

Louise Richardson Forrest

Illustrations by Denise Casey

Stackpole Books

Published by
STACKPOLE BOOKS
Cameron and Kelker Streets
P.O. Box 1831
Harrisburg, PA 17105

Printed in the United States of America

10 9 8 7 6 5 4 3 2 1

Library of Congress Cataloging-in-Publication Data

Forrest, Louise Richardson.
  Field guide to tracking animals in snow.

  Bibliography: p.
  Includes index.
  1. Tracking and trailing. 2. Animal tracks.
I. Casey, Denise. II. Title.
QL768.F67   1988   599   88-2153
ISBN 0-8117-2240-6

Dedication

*To the animals herein for all the hours of joy and
entertainment they have provided me.
May this book help give others a better understanding
of the importance of animals and of the loneliness
we would suffer without them.*

And to two special people: Steve and Tilsley.

Contents

Contents

Contents

Acknowledgments

Since I began collecting material for this book in 1982, many people have provided information about specific animals, and many have given assistance in a variety of areas. I wish to express my thanks to the following colleagues and friends for all their help, advice, and encouragement: Rich Anderson, Virginia Barber, Jeremy Betts, Steve Buskirk, Cate Cabot, Tom Campbell, Tim Clark, Ron Crete, Martha Collins, Mike Fairchild, Dennis Flath, Steve Forrest, James Halfpenny, Bruce and Molly Hampton, Deb and Jeff Jones, Barb Mangelsdorf, Steve Minta, Roger Powell, Bill Stanley, Julie Trapp, Gene Young, and my family.

In addition, a number of people generously sent me slides or photos, both for illustration references and for use in the book. For these I would like to thank Steve Amstrup (U.S. Fish and Wildlife Service—USFWS—polar bears); Steve Buskirk (University of Wyoming—wolverine, pine marten, shrews, voles, muskrats, and others); Tom Campbell (Biota Research and Consulting Inc.—pygmy rabbit); Tim Clark (Northern Rockies Conservation Cooperative—mountain lion); Harry Hartwell (Washington Department of Natural Resources—opossum and mountain beaver); Jim Hasbrouck (University of Iowa—raccoon); Jeff Jones (U.S. Forest Service—USFS—fisher); David Klein (Alaska Cooperative Wildlife Research Unit—caribou); Richard Richards (O & R Laboratories—ringtail); William Rich-

11

ardson (gray squirrel); Roger Smith (Teton Science School—black bear); and Robert Stephenson (Alaska Department of Fish and Game—lynx).

A few people also obtained track measurements or other information for me that has been most helpful and deeply appreciated. They were Tom Campbell (pygmy rabbit); Tim Clark (mountain lion); Scott Craven (University of Wisconsin, Extension—opossum); Lyle Crosby (USDA—Animal Damage Control—spotted skunk); Mike Fairchild (University of Montana—wolf); Dennis Flath (Montana Fish, Wildlife and Parks—least weasel); Craig Gardner (USFWS—polar bear, wolverine, and arctic fox); David Klein (caribou and muskox); Martin Raphael (USFS—least weasel); Lew Rosenbluth (rats); Mikael Sandell (University of Lund—least weasel); and Robert Stephenson (lynx). Many of the people who contributed material also reviewed parts of the manuscript, for which I am grateful.

Draft manuscripts were kindly reviewed by Robert Butterfield (National Park Service, NPS—Denali); Steve Buskirk, Tom Campbell, Tim Clark, Steve Forrest, James Halfpenny, Bruce Hampton, John Kansas (Beak Consultants, Calgary); Dick Randall (Defenders of Wildlife); Keith Smith (NPS—Acadia); John Varley, Norm Bishop, and Jospeh Zarki (NPS—Yellowstone). I would like to express my gratitude to them for their thoughtful, thorough, and helpful reviews.

I would especially like to thank Denise Casey for her superb illustrations, as well as her patience, advice, and friendship during this entire project.

L. R. F.

I would like to thank Kris Worl and Barbara Smith (Pioneer of Jackson Hole), and Erica Hansen Craig for technical assistance. The Peabody Museum of Natural History, New Haven, Connecticut, kindly permitted me to make drawings of some museum mounts. James Halfpenny took time from his busy schedule to review the preliminary sketches, and we both very much appreciate his help. And I especially thank Tim Clark, not only for his critiques of the drawings, but also for his support and encouragement.

D. C.

Introduction

Many people assume that in winter wild animals, like so many of us, escape the difficulties of traveling, feeding, and keeping warm by migrating or hibernating. This is true of cold-blooded animals and of many warm-blooded birds and mammals. However, a surprising number of birds and mammals conduct business as usual, and whenever they move, rest, feed, hunt, or behave in other ways on the ground, a record is impressed in the snow. Indeed, without the use of sophisticated equipment, snow offers one of the best opportunities to learn about the lives of animals in winter.

But why, you may ask, would anyone want to follow an animal around in the winter? Imagine a bright, sunny morning after a snow storm—air crisp, snow sparkling—a perfect day for a ski, a walk, or a snowmobile ride. Traveling into the woods or across the fields, you suddenly intersect a winding trail interrupting the snow's smooth surface. With a little imagination, you envision the trail-maker walking, waddling, or trotting along. You follow the trail and find numerous clues that reveal this animal's daily activities.

Perhaps the trail leads to the scene of a successful hunt where the two-print trail of a weasel slowed, disappeared under the snow, and then reappeared, accompanied by tiny drag marks of a hapless vole. It may lead to a spot marking the swoop of an unlucky hawk and the scurry of a luckier mouse; to a place where two coyotes met and continued on together; to a mysterious dead-end where a grouse took off in flight; to a small depression where a moose gently touched its nose to the snow to sniff for food; or to a hill that proved irresistible to sliding otters or mink. The trail itself, whether it meanders or strikes out straight ahead, reflects the behavior of the animal in motion and provides substantial amounts of biological data. More important, following it is fun! But please be aware that in winter animals are generally operating on very strict energy budgets. If you frighten them excessively or harass them, either by pursuing too closely on foot or following on a snowmobile, you may tip the scale between survival and death.

Why a book on snow-tracking when so many fine tracking books exist? During my first winter tracking efforts, I often found it difficult to match the tracks I saw in the snow with the detailed shape and toe counts of my track book illustrations. So often, snow obscured these foot details that are useful when identifying tracks in mud, sand, and sometimes in shallow snow. After several winters studying animals in the field, I decided to compile that information, gathered from my own experiences and from other track books, which proved most helpful for identifying tracks in snow.

I learned that the first rule of snow-tracking is to identify the animal's track pattern, the trail left in the snow, which is often identifiable even when the tracks are windblown and obscured. Consequently, this book emphasizes track patterns, although print details are always important tracking clues whenever visible.

Mammals are the prime focus of this book because their tracks are the ones most likely to be found in winter. Tracks of birds and domestic mammals are also discussed. The North American animals included in this book are primarily those that are active in winter in areas that commonly receive snow.

About Snow

How animals have adapted to life in snow country is fascinating. Let's take a closer look at that snow environment. Snow is not just snow. Arctic natives have a surprisingly large vocabulary to describe the various forms of snow and its structure within the snowpack. While some of these variations are caused above the snow by environmental conditions like wind and cold; others, more important to many animals, are caused from below.

In areas where a persistent snow cover occurs, the temperature of the ground surface closely parallels the outside air temperature until snow cover is deeper than 6 inches. With snow cover comes an insulating blanket that retards the natural loss of the earth's heat. As a result, the bottom of the snowpack becomes warmer than the top (which is exposed to cold air), and a thermal gradient is created in which heat and moisture flow upward. Snow crystals near the soil break down, and their water molecules migrate either to larger crystals or to those above.

Eventually, the bottom snow structure becomes a fragile latticework of large, coarse, granular crystals called depth hoar. This weak layer, often an underlying cause of avalanches, also provides many small animals a relatively warm, stable environment where they can easily burrow, travel, and nest while protected from the cold temperatures above. A dark, silent "undersnow" world is created with intricate systems of runways, tunnels, and burrows. Above, you trod along unaware of the world of activity below you! But if you are observant, you can find holes by trees or shrubs or openings near downed logs, brush piles, or rocks that are entryways to this subnivean (undersnow) world.

Of the animals that do not migrate or hibernate, only the larger ones are able to withstand extreme cold. The smaller mammals, such as shrews, voles, and mice, have such small body masses relative to their body surface area that their metabolism cannot maintain body warmth in freezing temperatures. They go below the snow where it rarely drops below 15°F. Even some spiders can remain active in this environment.

The subnivean air is saturated with moisture—a boon to shrews, which have poor mechanisms to control their body moisture. It is also ideal for scent communication in the hunting efforts of small predators. The difficult times for these small animals are spring and fall when temperatures are cold and the snowpack is beginning or ending.

Small weasels spend much of their time under the snow hunting rodents and using rodent runways and nests for their own.

Besides the fact that most of their prey live under the snow, these weasels must also seek shelter here because they have high rates of metabolism, small bodies, little fat, and fur of only moderate insulating value.

Red squirrels are also confined to the subnivean world at times. They make tunnels and runways to reach their cone caches near the soil, and nest under the snow when temperatures reach below about −25°F.

Large mammals have adapted to snow travel through modifications of the feet or legs. For example, the feet of the snowshoe hare and the lynx are large relative to body size. Other examples are the rounded, splayed hoofs of the caribou and the long, stilt-like legs of the moose. The moose's rear legs articulate so they can be inserted in snow and retracted at nearly the same angle.

When you travel on snow, it's fascinating to speculate on the ways animals manage to stay active in the winter and to look for clues to where and how they do it.

How to Use This Book

For each mammal or mammal group discussed in this book several types of information have been provided to help you identify the tracks: a description and illustration of the animal; a description of its habitat with a range map; and illustrations, descriptions, and measurements of the animal's tracks and associated signs. (Note that the scientific names of mammals are given in the species accounts and with the mammal's common name in the index.) Birds and domestic mammals are discussed in abbreviated form at the end.

When identifying an animal's track, I have found it most helpful first to identify the animal's track pattern. After reading the following discussion of track pattern types, use the mammal track pattern key located on the inside front cover (see pp. 28 and 29 for how to use it) or the track patterns shown in the bird section to help you match the pattern you see with the correct animal group. While doing this, think about what type of habitat the animal lives in. It will help narrow down your choices.

Finally, take a closer look at the animal's tracks and take a few measurements to decide specifically which animal you are tracking. Also, look along the animal's trail for other clues that may help you identify the animal. In just a short time, you will be able to recognize common tracks after a quick look. Note that all the track pattern illustrations in the animal accounts run up the right side of the right-hand page, making it easy to flip through these for quick reference.

If you are lucky enough to glimpse a mammal while tracking, the descriptions and illustrations in the book should help you identify it. The measurements given for each mammal are total length (body plus tail) and tail length. Weights are also given to help you estimate how deep the animal's track should be. Now let me discuss the steps to track identification in greater detail.

Steps to Track Identification

Step One: Identify the animal's track pattern

Taking a walk in the snow, you come upon a series of foot *prints* or *tracks* ahead of you. This series of tracks is the animal's *trail*. Looking more carefully, you notice that the trail has a *track pattern*, a distinctive arrangement of the tracks.

> • First, you need to identify which of the three main track patterns (summarized in the Key) the trail resembles. To do this, follow the trail for at least several yards in one or both directions to get a feel for the animal's most typical track pattern and to find additional clues to the animal's identity, such as scats (or pellets or droppings) or distinctive behaviors (does it climb, fly, or swim?). Perhaps what you first saw was a place where a rabbit slowed from its normal hopping gait to walk and explore a shrub. *When in doubt, follow the trail!* Here are the main track patterns.

The Alternating Track Pattern

The first type of track pattern animals make looks more or less like yours. Look behind you. As you walk, one track is made on the right, then another on the left, right, left, and so on. What you see are two parallel rows of tracks with the prints alternately spaced—an *alternating track pattern* (*a, b*). Although we produce this pattern by walking with two feet, when four-footed animals walk or trot slowly they produce the same pattern

●	Hind feet
○	Front feet
◖	Front and hind feet landing in same location

Key to identifying front and hind feet in track patterns described below.

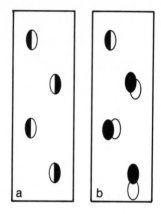

Alternating track pattern. **a.** *Alternating track pattern with hind-foot prints neatly registering on front-foot prints.* **b.** *Offset alternating track pattern with hind feet landing close to front-foot prints.*

An elk walking. Note how the hind foot lands where the opposing front foot previously stepped (drawn from Muybridge, 1979).

18

by placing their hind feet neatly in the tracks made by their front feet. Sometimes in shallow snow, an animal's hind feet fall slightly ahead, behind, or to the side of its front-foot prints, making an *offset alternating track pattern* (*b*). However, in deep snow, the animal saves energy by placing its hind feet in its front-foot tracks. Think about following a friend's tracks in deep snow. It's much easier to step in those tracks than to make your own.

All mammals and most birds *walk*, but more often mammals travel in other movement patterns or *gaits*. Other gaits include, in general order of increasing speed, *trotting*, *loping* (a slow gallop), *jumping* (a bounding or hopping gait), and *galloping*. Jumping is different from loping or galloping because movement off the feet occurs simultaneously and with equal force.

Some animals that commonly walk in snow, making an alternating track pattern, are the members of the bear, dog, and cat families, and the ungulates (hoofed mammals)—all of which are long-bodied and thus take long steps. Those walkers that are short-bodied (and take short steps) include opossums, beavers, muskrats, porcupines, badgers, skunks, lemmings, and ground-dwelling birds. Marmots, prairie dogs, and voles also fall in this group; however, they often move in a jumping gait. (Group members drag their bodies in soft, relatively shallow snow.) Members of the dog family and the ungulates sometimes trot when snow is shallow, maintaining the alternating track pattern but with longer steps. All these mammals occasionally gallop, but only for short stretches in snow.

The Two-print Track Pattern

The second major track pattern is the *two-print track pattern*, in which two tracks appear close together followed by a distinct space, then two more tracks (*c*, *d*, *e*). One type of two-print track pattern is made by members of the weasel or mustelid family (except badgers and skunks) when they lope (*c*). They move by leaping forward off their hind feet and landing with their front feet. Then the front feet leave the ground again before the hind feet finally land—on or near the front-foot prints (see illustration on next page). Usually, but not always, one of the two prints falls slightly behind the other. The prints are usually spaced close together, sometimes making a single two-lobed impression in the snow. Occasionally two pairs of tracks are connected by a trough

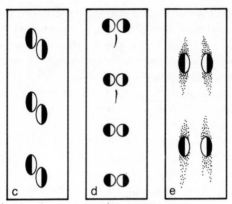

Some two-print track patterns. **c.** *Two-print loping track pattern made by most members of the weasel or mustelid family.* **d. and e.** *Paired two-print track patterns made by voles and mice (d) and chipmunks and tree squirrels (e). This occurs when their four-print group merges in soft snow.*

Short-tailed weasel loping. Its hind feet land together in the location previously occupied by the front feet (drawn from Gambaryan, 1974).

made by the animal's body.

In soft snow, mice, voles (*d*), chipmunks, tree squirrels, and tree-dwelling birds (*e*) make a two-print pattern in which the tracks are typically paired side by side. Except for birds, these short-bodied animals actually jump as they would to make a four-print pattern (described below) in shallow snow; however, the tracks merge to form a two-print pattern. Their bodies may also make troughs linking two sets of tracks. In the case of voles, this is a particularly common pattern. Tree-dwelling birds usually hop on the ground with their feet together.

Raccoons and opossums, short-legged and wide-bodied, make a two-print walking pattern in which the hind feet are placed next to the tracks of the opposing front feet (*f*). Thus, each two-print group contains prints of two sizes—one the print of the larger hind foot. The opossum's hind-foot track is particularly

20

distinctive because it shows a backward-pointing "thumb."

Some of the long-bodied walking mammals, particularly ungulates and dogs, make two-print track patterns when trotting in shallow snow. When the trot is fast, ungulates, especially, may completely overstep the front-foot prints with their hind feet,

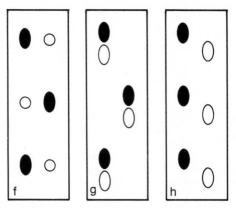

Other two-print track patterns. **f.** *Walking two-print track pattern made by raccoons and opossums.* **g. and h.** *Two-print trotting track patterns typical of the ungulates (g) and the dog family (h).*

making a two-print track pattern (*g*), really a very offset alternating track pattern. Another trotting pattern typical of the dog family shows a two-print pattern with the front-foot prints on one side of the imaginary centerline and the hind foot prints on the other side, behind, next to, or ahead of the front print, depending on speed (*h*).

The Four-print Track Pattern

The third major track pattern is the *four-print track pattern,* where four footprints are grouped together followed by a space and then four more prints (*i* and *j*). The most common type of four-print pattern is made by rodents and rabbits as they jump or hop. The animal jumps forward off its large muscular hind legs and lands on its front feet, placing them either side by side or slightly on a diagonal. Then it places its hind feet around the outside and ahead of its front-foot prints (see illustration). Tree dwellers place their front feet side by side most often (*i, bottom*), while ground dwellers usually place their front feet on a diagonal

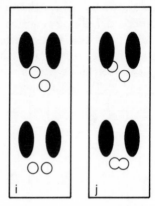

Common four-print track patterns. **i.** Four-print track patterns made by most rabbits and rodents when hopping; ground dwellers place their front feet on a diagonal (top), while tree dwellers place theirs side by side (bottom). **j.** Three-print variations of the four-print track pattern where a front-foot print merges with a hind-foot print or the front-foot prints merge together.

(*i, top*). This rule applies to mammals as well as to most birds.

During a four-print jump, the hind feet sometimes fall on top of one or both of the front-foot prints leaving only three or two prints showing (see two-print track patterns), or the two front feet land close together merging into one print (*j*). In the case of larger rodents and rabbits, both front prints rarely merge with the hind prints to form the two-print pattern made by small rodents in deep snow.

Four-print track patterns are also made when a mammal lopes or gallops, as shown; but, because of the energy it takes to move in snow, they are uncommon and typically seen only for short stretches. Those mammals that already jump in a four-print pat-

Tassle-eared squirrel hopping. Note how the hind feet are brought around and ahead of the front feet (drawn from Gambaryan, 1974).

tern merely extend their feet, maintaining the same pattern as speed increases. Basically, other mammals gallop by leaping off their hind feet, landing forward with their front feet, and then taking off from their front feet to create an airborne phase before the hind feet land again. A galloping track pattern is sometimes an indication that the animal was frightened—perhaps by you!

Loping and galloping four-print patterns vary, depending on the species of animal and its speed. The accompanying illustrations show slower lopes (k and l), and faster gallops (m, n, o). Lope k is typical of the dog family, while lope l is typical of mustelids. The C-shaped rotatory gallop (m) is common among the dog, deer, and antelope families. Dogs, mustelids, and un-

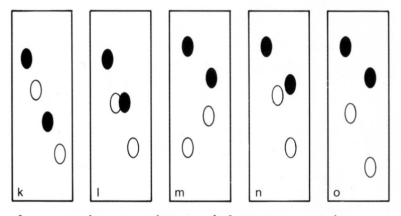

Less common four-print track patterns. **k.** *Loping pattern typical of the dog family.* **l.** *Loping pattern typical of mustelids.* **m.** *"C-shaped" rotatory gallop common among dogs, deer, and antelope.* **n.** *Faster galloping pattern.* **o.** *Most common galloping track pattern made by all mammals (drawn from Halfpenny, 1986).*

gulates commonly make gallop n. Gallop o is the most common galloping print made by almost all families of mammals. Mule deer exhibit their own variation of a jump called a "stot," jumping off all four legs at once in Pogo-stick-like movements and leaving a clustered four-print track group. (Much of this discussion on mammal gaits is taken from James Halfpenny's excellent book, *A Field Guide to Mammal Tracking in Western America*.)

• A final note on track patterns: Consider the character of the animal's movements. Does it travel erratically, moving in different directions (a weasel energetically investigating every spot)? Does it move purposefully forward, largely unconcerned with cover or habitat (a wolf or coyote on the move)? Do its movements lead from tree to tree (a tree squirrel, porcupine, or marten) or from burrow to burrow (a ground squirrel, prairie dog, or perhaps a black-footed ferret)? Or does it wander from shrub to shrub nibbling winter stems (a hare, elk, or moose)? An animal's trail holds many different clues to the animal's identity. These clues are described in the species accounts.

Step Two: Decide in which type of habitat the animal lives

• While identifying the basic track pattern of your mystery animal, think about where you are. Are you deep in a New England forest? A Minnesota riparian area (near a lake, pond, or stream)? Or maybe an "edge" between different habitat types? Some animals, such as prairie dogs and ground squirrels, are lovers of open, western prairies, while others, such as tree squirrels, require forest habitats. Still others, like coyotes, travel long distances through all types of terrain. Are you in the suburbs or the wilderness? A wolverine rarely visits the suburbs. When you look at the species accounts, make sure you look at both the habitat information and the range map that tell you which part of the country is home to each animal.

Step Three: Identify the animal

• Now is the time to move in on the track (but don't push snow over it!) and take a closer look. Look for additional clues (are there pads or claws?) and take a few measurements. When out in the woods or mountains in winter I often carry a small cloth tape measure, a notebook, and a camera for recording tracks. You may want to carry a ruler or use the one on the back cover of this guide, or you may prefer standby rulers—a hand or fingers. The stretch between my thumb and little finger across my palm measures about 8 inches. The tip joint of my index finger measures an inch. This often gives me the ballpark estimate I need to confirm a track or give me a general ideal about which one to look up in a track book later. More often than not, I recognize a certain track by its relative size compared to my hand or finger than by actual numbers I have memorized.

Track Shapes and Other Hints

• Although an animal's footprint is rarely perfectly detailed in snow, you often see the general foot shape, the overall track size and hints of toes, foot pads, or claws. It is important to remember that all the toes rarely register in a snow track, both because soft snow does not hold a print well and because the hind foot often falls where the front foot landed. Toe count is a major key to identifying tracks in many track books, and it can be useful in old or shallow snow as well as in dirt substrates, *but don't count on it.* For example, among three groups that walk making similar track patterns—dogs, cats and ungulates—the dogs can be distinguished by their elliptically shaped feet and traces of pad prints and claws. Cats have round feet with retractile claws, and ungulates have hoofs. In particularly soft, deep snow, even these features may be obscured, in which case you must look for other tracking clues or follow the trail to an area of shallower snow, for example under a tree branch.

Track Sizes

• Keep three things in mind before measuring tracks. First, tracks in snow are slightly larger than the actual foot size and sometimes larger than tracks of the same animal in mud or sand. Also, when the hind-foot print registers on the front-foot print, this track composite is slightly larger than you would expect a single footprint to be. The range of track measurements given in this book for each species group reflects these facts.

Second, *prints in snow change size with age.* A print exposed to warm sun may melt out to twice its original size after a couple of days. Gravity, freezing, and thawing break apart tracks; blowing snow or new snow fills in tracks. Use your own footprints to judge a track's freshness. Follow the trail to find tracks made in the shelter of trees or rocks, or on a different snow surface, to get a better idea of the real track size. Keep in mind that track sizes can vary with age of the track as well as with age and sex of the animal, and use the other clues—habitat, range, and associated signs—to help identify the track.

Finally, keep in mind that the depth of the print is a good indicator of an animal's size and weight. For example, lynx and mountain lion tracks are similar in size, but the lynx, very light for its large feet, rarely sinks deeply into snow. Look around your neighborhood to see the depth and size of the prints made by a local cat, dog, or other resident animal for a frame of reference.

• Track measurements given in this book include: (1) length and width of *single prints*, a track made by one foot or, in the alternating or two-print track patterns, by two feet when the hind foot registers on the front foot; (2) the length and width of the *print group*, the tracks made when each foot has touched down once, generally applicable to the two- and four-print track patterns (the print group in the alternating pattern does not occur as a distinct cluster); (3) the distance between each single print or print group, called the *intergroup* distance or length; and (4) the *straddle*, the width between the outermost prints or the width of the trail (*p* and *q*). (The distance from the trailing end of one print group to the trailing end of the next group, one full step cycle, is commonly called a stride.)

When measuring single prints or print groups, measure be-

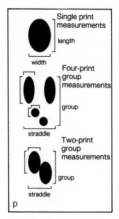
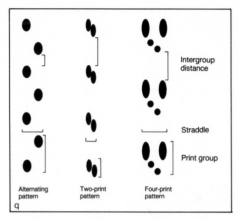

Standard track measurements. (Note: in the alternating pattern, use the distance between any two prints as the intergroup distance.)

tween the widest or longest points and just where the animal's foot stepped down (the flat part of the track), excluding the outer edges of the track or places where the foot slid through the snow before or after it stepped down. When claw marks are visible, include them in the print length measurement. To measure the intergroup distance, measure the distance between any two consecutive print groups. Note that in the alternating pattern, the print group can be a set of any two prints. In this case, consider the distance between any two prints as the intergroup distance.

The straddle indicates the width of the animal and is often a good way to distinguish between two members of a family that move in the same manner, such as between deer, elk, and moose. In general, as an animal increases speed, the print group length increases and the straddle decreases. However, the straddle often increases when an animal moves into deep snow. The intergroup distance may actually decrease when some animals increase their gait.

Always take several measurements, averaging them until you obtain a general range of measurements to compare with the range of sizes for each measurement in the book. Measuring one or two unusually long leaps made by a tree squirrel or only one or two fox prints could prove puzzling, but measuring several tracks along the trail will give a more accurate picture of which animal you are tracking. *When in doubt, follow the trail.*

Finally, *focus on measurements that are least variable.* For example, the straddle is typically less variable than the intergroup distance. Look in the section introducing each mammal group for the discussion of those measurements most helpful for distinguishing between the mammals in that group.

Associated Signs

• The signs an animal leaves along its trail are excellent clues to the animal's identity. These signs include *scats* or *pellets*; resting *beds* where the animal lay down to rest during the day or night; *evidence of feeding* where the animal stopped to browse or perhaps feed on another animal; *scent marks* where the animal rubbed or scratched, often in association with *urination*; and *hair.* The signs found most often in winter for each species or species group are described in the species accounts. In many cases, signs are frequently seen along trails, and they enliven the story of the animal you are tracking.

How to Use the Track Pattern Key

An abbreviated key to the mammal track patterns discussed above is located on the inside front cover. It will help you select the proper mammal group, family or species, according to track patterns.

• After reading through the introduction, start identifying your mystery track by looking at the track patterns diagrammed on the left side of the page, noting some of the possible variations in the basic pattern itself.

• Once you determine the animal's track pattern, review the choices that help you separate the animals into different groups by size or shape. For example, if the trail shows an alternating track pattern, you must decide whether the animal is long- or short-bodied—that is, whether or not the intergroup distance is generally longer or shorter than 8 or 9 inches. If it is long-bodied, you are directed to one of four families. Using clues in the Key, you decide, for instance, that your animal is in the dog family.

• Then, go to the page number for that section of the book and use the additional information there on habitat, range, shape and size of tracks, and associated signs to make your final decision. Keep in mind the potential for irregularity and assess several tracks or track groups before you decide.

• An asterisk (*) in the Key warns of animals that commonly vary their gait. A few animals, such as the voles, actually appear in more than one track pattern group. Not included in the Key are gaits that are uncommon for a particular animal and that would only be seen for a short distance—for example, the walking alternating track pattern for the hopping rabbit or the loping weasel.

• The galloping gaits listed at the bottom of the Key are uncommon in deep snow because they require much energy. You may see them occasionally in shallow snow over frozen ground or ice, especially in the case of larger animals; however, most animals cannot keep up this gait for long. Therefore, at the risk of being redundant, *follow the trail!* At least in shallow snow, you are likely to see a detailed print to help identify the animal.

Direction of Travel

People often wonder how to determine which way an animal is going—something that may be important if you wish to observe (or perhaps avoid!) an animal. Look for partial toe or claw prints, which point in the direction of travel. The shape of the foot can help you tell where the front of the track is. For example, the hind foot of most weasels and rodents is broadest across the front, tapering down to a narrower heel. The snow is often more compressed at the front of the track where more weight is placed. Foot placement is also important. When rabbits and rodents bound, they usually place their hind feet ahead of their front feet, so that the hind feet are actually leading the tracks.

Finally, when an animal walks either on the flat or downhill, it often slides its feet into the print trough, steps, and then lifts them out. The result is a trough in the snow, longer and shallower where the foot entered, and steeper and more abrupt where the foot was lifted out—or toward the direction the animal was traveling. The movement pattern uphill is often reversed because the animal lifts its legs high to step into the snow and then drags them out as it moves forward. This movement may throw snow forward too.

Preserving Tracks

Besides making various field notes about tracks, I generally preserve tracks with photographs. Tracks are best photographed in direct sunlight with the print an inch or more deep. Position yourself so the sun casts shadows in the print, adding depth and contrast against the snow. On a bright day, I sometimes use a polarizing filter to help cut the glare from the snow, or I underexpose the photo a little. Shoot at a couple of exposure readings to see what works best with the particular film you are using. (Make sure you have some scheme to remember which shot was which.) Including a pencil, lens cap, notebook, foot, body, or ruler in the photo helps give scale to the tracks. Shoot at least one photo aiming straight down at the print and scale item if possible. This alleviates any distortion caused by shooting at an angle and allows you to take measurements from your slide later. Your camera should be as close to the print as your focus will allow, filling the frame.

It's also possible to make plaster casts of tracks in snow. You will need: temperatures below freezing; a spray bottle (such as that used to humidify plants); plaster of paris; a mixing container; and water. Spray the track with a mist of water (if the water doesn't come out in a fine mist, it will break apart the track). Allow it to freeze. Mix some plaster of paris with water to the consistency of a slightly thick pancake batter. Be careful not to make it too thick, otherwise it will set up too quickly, preventing a good flow into all the nooks and crannies of the track. If it's too thin or too warm, it will break through your ice mold. If the water has warmed up, mix it with snow to cool it down as much as possible. You may need to form a barrier of snow or to use a cardboard ring held together with a paper clip to prevent the plaster from flowing out of the track. After you fill the print with plaster, overflowing it slightly, let it set for a good ten minutes or more before removing the cast. Heavy, wet snow provides the bese chance for good track detail, while soft, powder snow proves frustrating to casting efforts.

Opossum Family: Didelphidae

Only one species of marsupial (order Marsupialia) lives north of Mexico, the Virginia opossum in the opossum family (Didelphidae), and it has shown itself to be successful in most habitats except those that are very cold or very dry. Historically an inhabitant of the southeastern United States, the opossum is now widely distributed in the north and west as well.

Opossums have an abdominal pouch (a marsupium) in which the nipples are located and where the young, born after a very short gestation period, nurse and develop after birth. They also have long, narrow jaws containing small incisors, large canines, and sharp molars, and a naked, prehensile tail.

Omnivorous, solitary, and nocturnal, these southerners are poorly adapted to subzero temperatures, which frostbite their ears and tails. Consequently, where winters are severe, they put on fat in fall and den up during cold weather in ground burrows abandoned by other animals, in rock crevices, stumps, tree hollows, brush piles, or old buildings.

Opossums usually walk, making two different track patterns. One is an alternating pattern in which the hind feet fall slightly behind the front-foot prints of the same side. Tracks in this pattern can be confused with those of a muskrat when accompanied by a tail drag. However, muskrat tracks have smaller foot widths, straddles, and intergroup lengths, and they rarely occur on snow and then only near water. In light or wet snow, opossum tracks show a distinctive, nearly backward-pointing "thumb" on the hind foot.

The other walking pattern resembles that of the raccoon. This is a two-print pattern in which the hind feet fall next to the opposing front-foot prints. In firm or light snow, the opossum tracks are more splayed and show thumbs. In soft, deep snow, the two tracks are quite similar, but the opossum trail has a long, thin tail drag mark resembling that of the muskrat.

1"

OPOSSUM
Didelphis virginiana

Description: The size of a large, stout house cat, opossums are slow-moving, grayish animals with long, naked tails and short legs. Total length averages 30 inches and tails are about 12 inches long. Adults weigh 9 to 13 pounds.

Habits: Although they occupy a wide variety of habitats, opossums prefer woody or brushy stream bottoms, swamps, and lakeshores in lowland areas. They are also commonly found in agricultural and suburban areas, and are highly omnivorous, feeding on small animals, garbage, and carrion. Adept climbers, they are solitary and nocturnal.

Track Pattern: Opossums are not well adapted to cold temperatures and den up in severe winter weather. When they emerge onto snow during thaws or in spring or fall, they walk placing their hind feet slightly behind their front-foot prints in an alternating track pattern (*a*) or placing their hind feet next to their opposing front feet, making a two-print track pattern (*b*). In old, wet, or light snow, the unusual "thumb" on the hind foot is unmistakable. A long, thin tail drag is present in soft or fresh snow.

Associated Signs: Few other signs of the opossum will be found in winter. However, the tail drag may sometimes include blood stains—evidence of a ragged and frostbitten tail. Scats are not particularly distinctive.

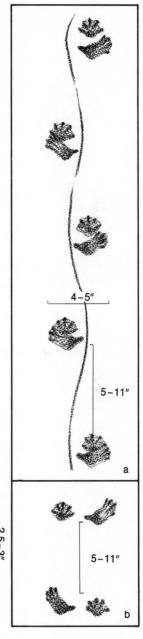

4–5"

5–11"

a

5–11"

b

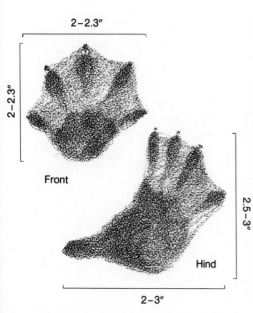

2–2.3"

2–2.3"

Front

2.5–3"

Hind

2–3"

37

Shrew Family: Soricidae

The smallest of mammals, shrews (family Soricidae) of the order Insectivora are almost constantly active, day or night, in their search for food to fuel their high metabolism. Furred with thick, soft coats, shrews have pointed snouts, reduced but visible eyes, short ears, and a row of small, sharp teeth extending along the length of the jaw—a different arrangement from rodent jaws that contain two long front incisors separated from their short cheek teeth.

Shrews are solitary and secretive. They are widespread throughout North America, especially where vegetation provides adequate cover and shelter. Some species move about on top of the ground, while others use subterranean tunnels or are nearly aquatic. At least fifteen shrew species inhabit the snow country of North America. Some species, like masked shrews, water shrews, arctic shrews, and pygmy shrews, range throughout northern U.S., Canada, and Alaska. Others, like Pacific water shrews and Gaspé shrews, have very limited ranges.

Come winter, many shrew species become members of the bustling, dark subnivean (undersnow) world. Here, a vast network of snow tunnels, made primarily by small rodents and connected with natural openings under logs, stumps, and roots, harbors a host of small animals and their predators, such as small mustelids. These networks are entered through holes by tree stems, log debris, squirrel caches, rocks, or buildings. Many shrews make globular nests of dried grasses and leaves in these snow tunnels, in shallow underground tunnels, or under protected surface features such as logs or rocks. One exception is the water shrew that nests in the banks of streams and lakes or in old beaver and muskrat houses. Shrews primarily eat insects (often in larval or pupal stages in winter) and other invertebrates. They also eat other animals, such as mice and other shrews, if they can be subdued, and carrion.

Shrews aren't above wintering indoors. One winter, while doing wildlife research, my husband and I lived in a cabin that came with its own resident shrew. It served us by apparently keeping mice away, being very discreet about garbage it would forage, and annihilating dormant flies living between the logs. It was a nervous and timid creature, but it could never resist cat food, even when it was quietly offered on the tip of a finger.

Members of the shrew family make a similar track pattern, although it varies slightly in size between the tiny pygmy shrews and the large northern short-tailed and water shrews. Shrew trails often show a four-print jumping pattern; however, in soft snow the hind- and front-foot prints may merge to form a two-print track pattern with tails dragging. Occasionally, shrews slow to a walk and make an alternating track pattern, often with erratic steps, but they usually break into a bounding gait again within a short distance.

Shrew trails are similar to but usually smaller and more variable than mice trails, and smaller than the variable vole trails. For most shrew species, the straddle is the key measurement for distinguishing between the larger mice and voles, although as a more subtle distinction, the shrews' hind feet do not seem to reach as far beyond their front feet as do those of mice or voles. Nevertheless, several straddle measurements usually tell you whether or not you're tracking the energetic shrew.

Moles (family Talpidae) are also in the order Insectivora, but because of their subterranean habits, their tracks in snow are highly unusual and are not included in this book.

SHREWS
Soricidae

0.5"

Description: Diminutive and voracious, shrews range in color from gray to brown to black and have hind feet larger than their front feet. Total length ranges from 3 to 7 inches, the tail from 0.5 to 3 inches. Shrews weigh 0.1 to 0.8 ounces.

Habits: In mid to northern North America, shrews live amidst dense vegetation in moist areas, often in woodlands, but they also inhabit alpine and arctic areas and open grasslands. They are active all year for short periods day or night—more often at night—feeding primarily on insects but also on other small animals. Except for the aquatic water shrews, most shrews are terrestrial and solitary.

Track Pattern: Shrews typically bound in a four-print track pattern with front feet often, but not always, diagonally placed. The four-print track merges to a two-print or a U-shaped track (*upper a*) in soft, deep snow. Occasionally, shrews slow to a walk making an erratic alternating pattern (*lower a*). Tails drag in soft, loose snow. Follow a shrew's trail and look for a place where it disappeared down an entryway to the subnivean world. Water shrews may have track measurements larger than shown, almost the size of mice or vole tracks.

Associated Signs: Infrequently, you may find small, dark, elongated shrew scats along a trail or on a cabin windowsill. You may also find where a tiny shrew has tunneled through snow for a short distance.

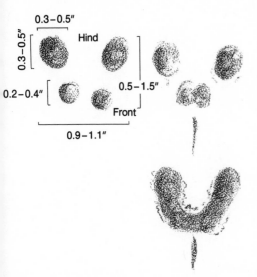

Rabbit Order: Lagomorpha

The pika (Ochotonidae) and rabbit (Leporidae) families of the order Lagomorpha are only distant relatives of rodents. The rabbit family is separated further into two groups, rabbits (*Sylvilagus* species) and hares (*Lepus* species). Rabbits, as distinct from hares, are born blind, naked, and helpless. Hares, including jackrabbits, are born with eyes open, fully haired, and are able to run within minutes after birth. Both rabbits and hares have relatively long hind legs and ears, furred soles, and short, fluffy tails.

Primarily diurnal (active by day) and solitary in winter, pikas are elfin rock lords, proclaiming their territories with loud *eeeps*, which anyone traveling in the western mountains hears long before spotting the diminutive creature—a gray, furry ball perching atop a boulder or scurrying among the rocks. Like the fabled ant, the pika prepares well for winter, cutting dried vegetation in summer and fall and storing it in "hay stacks" under boulders. Grassy nests tucked safely under rocks give the pika, which remains active all winter, little reason to venture beyond its rocky domain onto the snow. Nevertheless, it will soak up warm winter sunshine on an exposed boulder.

In spring, pikas move away from their rock shelters to find mates and new food supplies. This is the best time to find tracks, melted out snow tunnels, and winter scat piles, although fall snows also provide tracking opportunities. Pika tracks may be confused with those of red squirrels or chipmunks sharing the same habitat, but pika tracks are rounder, often merge into a three-print pattern, and are not found far from the rocks. Differences between species of North American pikas are primarily range and appearance. Habits and signs are similar.

Rabbits, hares, and their tracks are familiar to many people. These mammals are generally nocturnal and crepuscular (active at dawn and dusk), although they are occasionally seen by day. They are active year-round, solitary or in small groups and, except for pygmy rabbits, do not make underground dens. Instead, they rest by day in sheltered "forms," small depressions in the snow or ground, from which they explode in a flurry of fur and snow when surprised. White-tailed and black-tailed jackrabbits are also fond of resting in old badger burrows, and arctic hares sometimes den in short snow tunnels with enlarged chambers.

In winter, most rabbits and hares nibble on dry grass or the twigs, bark, and buds of sapling trees and shrubs. They nip twigs 1 to 2 feet off the ground at a clean 45-degree angle, which distinguishes a rabbit nibble from the untidy ripping of animals such as deer.

Although rabbit tracks are similar to those of some rodents, particularly squirrels, they are considerably larger. The most useful measurements for distinguishing between rabbit species are straddle and hind-foot width. In snow deeper than 3 to 4 inches, the lower hind leg of a rabbit or hare sinks into the snow, extending the hind foot track 1 to 2 inches. Don't confuse foot length with this handle-like extension, and be sure to use habitat and range information when track measurements of various rabbit species overlap. For example, European hares, Alaska hares, arctic hares, and jackrabbits all have tracks quite similar in size; but these species are found in very different habitats (also true of cottontail species). Be aware that some species have been introduced into areas outside of their range, mainly for hunting purposes.

All members of these two families have furred or mostly furred soles obscuring their foot pads. They typically hop or jump, making a characteristic four-print track pattern in which the larger hind feet fall ahead of the front-foot prints. Trailing a rabbit in snow is particularly entertaining because so much happens along the way. It's easy to find places where rabbits eat, rest, meet and, to another animal's good fortune, are sometimes attacked and eaten.

PIKAS
Ochotona species

0.5"

Description: Pikas or conies are small, gray, rabbit-like creatures with furry soles and no apparent tail. Compared to rabbits, their hind feet are rounder and not as large relative to their front feet. Total length is 6.5 to 8.5 inches, and weight is 4 to 6 ounces.

Habits: Pikas live in rocky, mountainous areas, such as boulder fields, rock slides, and cliff bases, either in exposed areas or in forest openings. Spaces between rocks must be large enough to provide pikas with travel corridors. Pikas are solitary in winter and feed on stored plants. They are active by day.

48

Track Pattern: In winter, pikas prefer to move among rocks or under snow, not on top of snow. Therefore, pika tracks are rarely found then. In fall or spring, look for fragments of a shuffling alternating track pattern or a short stretch of a three- or four-print bounding pattern (*a*). You are likely to hear the pika's startling, loud *eeep* and see it perched on a boulder much more often than you find its tracks.

Associated Signs: Investigate a pika's rock lair as snow melts and you are likely to find remnants of its winter "hay stacks" or see its tiny, black, B-B-like pellets. These may be in small groups among rocks or in large groups in melted-out runways among the rocks.

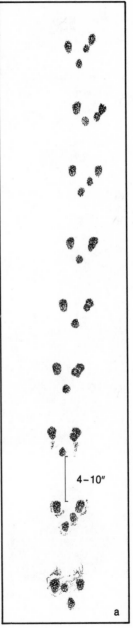

a

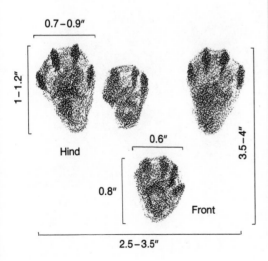

0.7–0.9"

1–1.2"

Hind

0.6"

0.8"

Front

3.5–4"

2.5–3.5"

4–10"

PYGMY RABBITS
Sylvilagus idahoensis

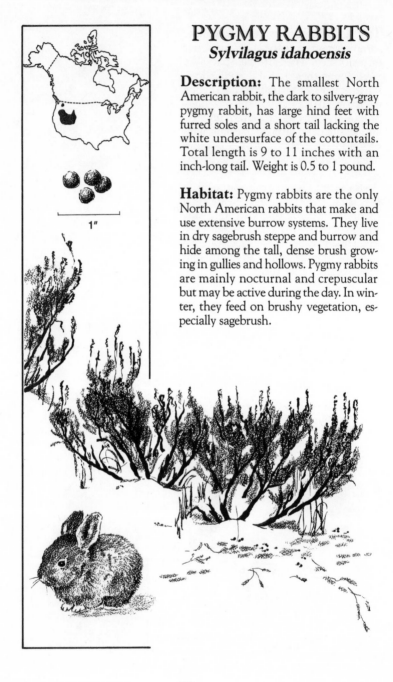

Description: The smallest North American rabbit, the dark to silvery-gray pygmy rabbit, has large hind feet with furred soles and a short tail lacking the white undersurface of the cottontails. Total length is 9 to 11 inches with an inch-long tail. Weight is 0.5 to 1 pound.

Habitat: Pygmy rabbits are the only North American rabbits that make and use extensive burrow systems. They live in dry sagebrush steppe and burrow and hide among the tall, dense brush growing in gullies and hollows. Pygmy rabbits are mainly nocturnal and crepuscular but may be active during the day. In winter, they feed on brushy vegetation, especially sagebrush.

1"

Track Pattern: Pygmy rabbits jump in a typical rabbit four-print track pattern with their hind feet placed ahead of their front feet (*a*), but their track measurements are considerably smaller than those of other rabbits. Sometimes the front-foot tracks merge to form a three-print pattern. Trails in snow can be found among dense brush nearly all winter except during severe weather.

Associated Signs: Pygmy rabbits leave spherical, fibrous pellets at the bases of tall brush. This often indicates the presence of a nearby concealed burrow entrance (4 to 5 inches wide). Other signs include twigs cut at a neat 45° angle about a foot off the ground. Look for the rabbits themselves hiding or resting in the brush.

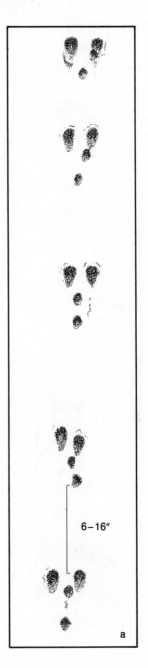

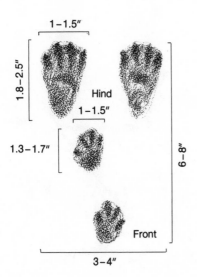

51

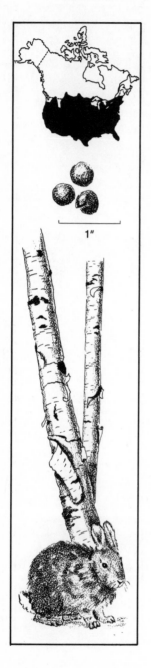

1"

COTTONTAIL RABBITS
Other *Sylvilagus* species

Description: These gray to brown medium-sized rabbits have partially or totally white "cotton puff" tails, large hind feet, and long hind legs. Total length varies by species from 12 to 18 inches with the tail 1 to 3 inches long. Weight is 1.3 to 4 pounds.

Habits: In eastern North America, cottontails live in heavy brush areas or dense boreal forests, while in the west they are found in brushy areas, as well as in open, dry shrublands and grasslands. Winter foods include bark, twigs, and woody vegetation. Cottontails are active all winter, except during severe weather, and are somewhat solitary, nocturnal, and crepuscular.

Track Pattern: Like other lago-morphs, cottontails jump making a four-print track pattern, their larger hind feet landing ahead of their front feet (*a*). Sometimes the front-foot prints merge with each other or with the hind-foot prints to make a three-print track group. The hind legs may sink into soft, deep snow, creating about an inch-long han-dle on the hind-foot prints.

Associated Signs: Cottontails typi-cally leave round, fibrous pellets at rest-ing and feeding sites, and they neatly clip buds and twigs within a foot or two of the ground. Their winter nests are usually depression-like forms concealed in brush or grass or in abandoned burrows of other animals. It is not uncommon to have one explode from under your feet when you pass by its hidden resting site.

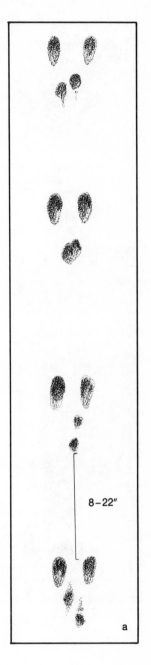

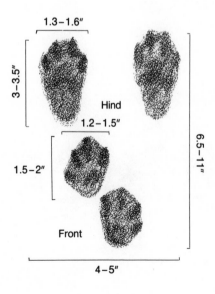

1.3–1.6"

3–3.5"

Hind

1.2–1.5"

1.5–2"

6.5–11"

Front

4–5"

8–22"

a

1"

SNOWSHOE HARE
Lepus americanus

Description: In winter, snowshoe hares, or varying hares, grow particularly thick fur on the soles of their hind feet, making "snowshoes" well-suited to snow travel. Pelage turns white in winter except for black-tipped ears. Total length is 15 to 21 inches, tail is 1 to 2 inches, and weight is 2 to 4 pounds.

Habits: Snowshoe hares live in brushy thickets in coniferous or mixed hardwood-conifer forests where they rest in forms under the cover of downed or standing trees and shrubs. Winter foods include twigs, bark, buds, and leaves of evergreen saplings or shrubs. These hares are active all winter, mainly nocturnal and crepuscular, and more gregarious than other hares.

Track Pattern: Snowshoe hares jump making the four-print track pattern typical of rabbits, except that the hind feet are nearly twice the size of the front feet (*a*). When snow is soft and deep, these hares often pack trails and runways through the brush. Because this hare's four-print group may extend up to 40 inches at top speed, you may only see the two hind or front prints at first. Make sure to stand back and look for the entire track group.

Associated Signs: Round, fibrous, light-brown pellets are often found near resting or feeding sites. Snowshoe hares clip twigs or buds at a neat 45° angle 1 to 2 feet off the ground. Following their tracks, you are likely to find a resting form in the brush nearby—or a brief glimpse of the hare you just scared away!

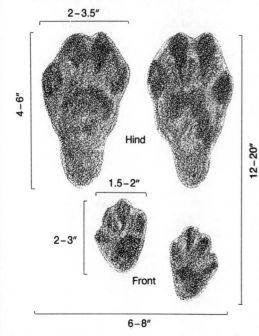

2–3.5"

4–6"

Hind

1.5–2"

2–3"

Front

6–8"

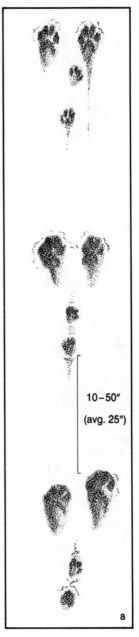

12–20"

10–50"

(avg. 25")

a

JACKRABBITS AND OTHER HARES
Lepus species

Description: This group includes arctic (*Lepus arcticus*) and Alaska (*L. othus*) hares and white-tailed jackrabbits (*L. townsendii*), which turn white in winter, as well as black-tailed jackrabbits (*L. californicus*) and European hares (*L. capensis*), which lighten but never turn white. All have long hind legs and large hind feet. Total length ranges from 19 to 27 inches with the tail 1.5 to 4.5 inches. Weight is 3 to 12 pounds.

Habits: White-tailed jackrabbits prefer open foothills, grasslands, and shrublands. Black-tails prefer drier areas but are spreading into white-tail habitat. Arctic and Alaska hares live in open arctic tundra, and European hares inhabit open hills and open hardwood forests. All eat woody plant parts in winter, are mainly nocturnal and crepuscular, and are active during the winter.

Track Pattern: These hares make a four-print jumping track pattern (*a*) similar to that of snowshoe hares, except that the hind feet are smaller. Also, the track group of the speedy jackrabbits (with leaps to 10 feet!) is often more extended. When the hind legs sink into deep snow, they create a 2-inch or larger extension to the hind-foot prints. Oddly enough, arctic hares may hop briefly on two hind feet when alarmed. Black-tailed jackrabbit tracks, the smallest of this group, are at the lowest size range shown.

Associated Signs: Signs of hares include round, brown, fibrous pellets left near feeding and resting sites, neatly clipped twigs 1 to 2 feet from the ground, and resting forms in snow. On prairies, watch for the flattened ears and back of a jackrabbit hiding in the shelter of an old badger burrow.

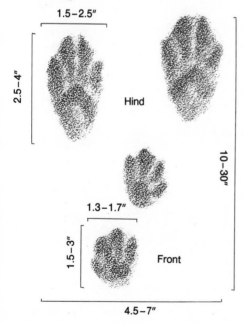

1.5–2.5"

2.5–4"

Hind

1.3–1.7"

1.5–3"

Front

10–30"

4.5–7"

10–60"
(avg. 20")

a

57

Rodent Order: Rodentia

Although the mere suggestion of rodents evokes a trembling horror in some people, you can't help but respect their remarkable evolutionary diversity. No other group has adapted so well to such a variety of environments. Technically, rodents have two large front incisors, excellent for nibbling and gnawing, and a space, the diastema, between their incisors and cheek teeth. The rodent order includes mountain beavers (family Aplodontiidae), chipmunks, marmots, squirrels (Sciuridae), beavers (Castoridae), New World mice, woodrats, voles, muskrats, lemmings (Cricetidae), Old World mice and rats (Muridae), and porcupines (Erethizontidae). North American families not discussed in this book, because you are not likely to see their tracks in snow, include pocket gophers (Geomyidae), which primarily live underground and tunnel under snow leaving a network of dirt tunnel cores or eskers, after snow melt. Also not discussed are antelope squirrels (Sciuridae), pocket mice, most kangaroo rats and mice (Heteromyidae), and jumping mice (Zapodidae)—all inactive for long periods in cold weather.

It is difficult to generalize about rodents because their behavior is so diverse. While chipmunks, marmots, prairie dogs, and ground squirrels hibernate in winter, their tree squirrel cousins remain active—a clue to squirrel track identification. Most squirrels are active during the day, except for the nocturnal flying squirrels. Mice, woodrats, and kangaroo rats are also nocturnal, but voles and mountain beavers are active by day or night.

Other rodent habits vary considerably. Many rodents are arboreal, while others, such as ground squirrels, kangaroo rats, lemmings, and most voles, are terrestrial. Still others, aquatic beavers and muskrats, spend most of their lives in or near the water. Wherever rodents live, they attract a host of predators—an important tracking clue.

Some rodents are highly gregarious and live in large social colonies—for example, prairie dogs and several of the ground squirrels. Others, such as beavers and muskrats, live in small family groups, while some mice and voles huddle for warmth in winter with family members or even members of other mice or vole species. Some, such as woodrats and porcupines, are solitary.

Rodents are generally herbivorous, with exceptions. Some ground squirrels eat carrion and have no qualms about nibbling on the body of a recently killed neighbor. Most interesting are carnivorous grasshopper mice, pint-sized predators whose diet includes invertebrates and even other mice and voles.

Most rodents jump making a four-print track pattern; their straddle and hind-foot widths are usually the best measurements for telling the rodents apart. Where there is potential for confusion (for example, between tree and ground squirrels or between tree-climbing mice and ground-dwelling voles), it helps to know that tree dwellers typically place their front feet paired side by side, while ground dwellers tend to place their front feet on a diagonal to the direction of travel, one behind the other. One group whose four-print pattern and straddle width are similar includes chipmunks, woodrats, and rats. In this case, you must look at the habitat and associated signs for identifying clues.

Sometimes the four-print pattern merges to a two-print pattern in soft snow, especially with smaller rodents. In that case, it helps to follow the trail to shallower or firmer snow. Voles often jump, forming a two-print pattern whatever the snow conditions. Their trails are best distinguished from those of mice by their long intergroup lengths.

Some larger rodents and lemmings walk rather than jump, making an alternating track pattern. These include mountain beavers, beavers, muskrats, porcupines, and occasionally, marmots and prairie dogs. Lemmings may also make a four-print loping pattern, unique among rodents but common to carnivores and ungulates. Straddle widths among these walkers are diagnostic, and where widths overlap, the species' habitats and associated signs resolve most confusion. It may be possible to confuse muskrat tracks with those of opposums because they both make long, thin, serpentine tail drag marks. However, the intergroup lengths and straddle widths of muskrat tracks are smaller, and muskrat trails rarely extend long distances on land or far from aquatic habitat.

MOUNTAIN BEAVER
Aplodontia rufa

Description: Resembling a thick-bodied, tailless muskrat, the mountain beaver is not a true beaver and is not always found in the mountains. Also called aplodontia or sewellel, this animal has coarse, dark-brown fur and short legs. Total length is 12 to 18 inches with a 1 inch tail. Mountain beavers weigh 2 to 3 pounds.

Habits: Mountain beavers dig extensive burrow systems in forests or dense thickets, principally at lower elevations. In winter, they tunnel through snow, extending their burrow systems to forage for bark and twigs. They are solitary and active at any time.

Track Pattern: Mountain beavers reduce their aboveground activity considerably in fall and winter. When they venture out of their burrows onto the snow, they walk making a short-stepped alternating track pattern (*a*), often offset in shallow snow. Their trails typically run between burrows and nearby trees and shrubs.

Associated Signs: Mountain beaver burrows have entrances 4 to 10 inches wide, sometimes with mounds of dirt or small piles of vegetation deposited near the opening, although most cuttings are carried below. Scats are also deposited below. Mountain beavers mark nearby young trees when they cut twigs and gnaw on bark. In spring, look for remnants of winter snow tunnels, about the width of burrow entrances.

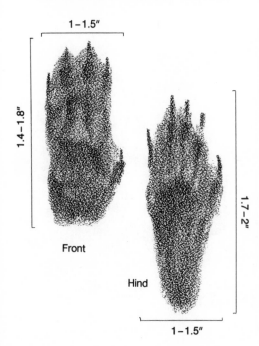

1–1.5"

1.4–1.8"

Front

Hind

1.7–2"

1–1.5"

2.5–3.5"

1–4"

a

63

CHIPMUNKS
Tamias species

Description: Varying in color from gray to brown to red, the sprightly chipmunks have alternating dark and light stripes along their backs and the sides of their heads. They have larger hind feet than front feet and tails of moderate length. Total length ranges from 7 to 11 inches with the tail 3 to 5 inches long. Weights range from 1 to 4.5 ounces.

Habits: Chipmunks live in partially wooded or brushy habitats and are primarily terrestrial, although they will climb trees. Generally solitary, they are active by day and make small, shallow burrows in the ground in which they nest and store seeds and other plant material for winter.

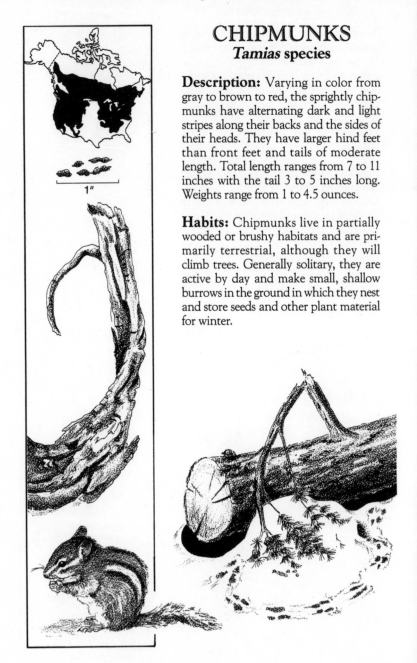

1"

Track Pattern: Chipmunks retire to their burrows and become torpid from October or November to February or March depending on species and area, except least chipmunks (*Tamias minimus*), which retire from September or October to April or May. They arise occasionally to feed on stores and may emerge in warm spells. They jump in a four-print track pattern with diagonally placed front feet (*a*). The large eastern chipmunks (*Tamias striatus*) may make tracks slightly larger than shown. Note variations in soft snow (*b*, *c*).

Associated Signs: If you see chipmunk tracks, you are likely to glimpse the chipmunk itself perching alertly on a fallen log or streaking toward its small—about 2-inch-wide— burrow. Other signs are rarely seen in winter.

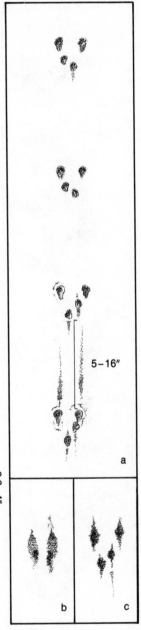

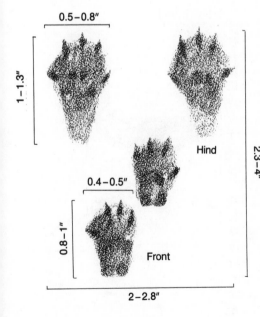

Hind

Front

65

Woodchucks

Marmots

Hoary Marmot

1"

MARMOTS
Marmota species

Description: Marmot species, often called rockchucks, woodchucks, groundhogs, or whistle-pigs, are large, corpulent squirrels with short legs. Pelage is dark-brown to red- or yellow-brown. Total length is 17 to 31 inches with the tail 4 to 10 inches. Weight is 5 to 20 pounds.

Habits: Relatively solitary, woodchucks (*Marmota monax*) prefer open woodlands or meadow edges in the east and den in the ground. The colonial western marmots prefer rock slides, rock outcrops, and meadows in mountainous regions and den among rocks or in the ground. All are diurnal herbivores and, although they can climb, are mainly terrestrial.

Track Pattern: Marmots put on fat in fall and hibernate in winter, from as long as September to April for the hoary marmot (M. *caligata*) to just October to February or March for the woodchuck. In spring and sometimes fall, look for the marmot's four-print jumping track pattern with diagonally placed front feet (*lower a*) or their lazier alternating walking pattern (*upper a*). Tracks of the large hoary marmot may be slightly larger than shown.

Associated Signs: Western marmot tracks lead to dens and sunning boulders where one often finds scats. Eastern woodchucks dig a well-known ground burrow (6 to 12 inches wide) with or without excavated dirt showing. Here, they sun themselves and leave scats nearby. Marmots and woodchucks announce your visit with sharp alarm whistles.

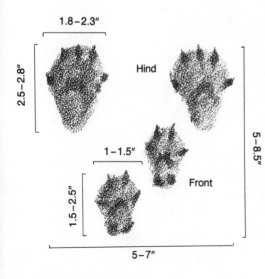

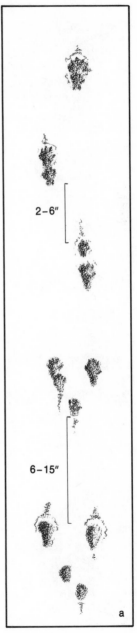

67

GROUND SQUIRRELS
Spermophilus **species**

Description: Often called gophers, "chislers," or "picket pins," ground squirrels are colored various shades of gray or brown with either plain, dappled, or striped backs. Hind feet are larger than front feet. Total length varies from 7 to 20 inches with a tail 2 to 10 inches. Weight is 6 to 40 ounces.

Habits: Most ground squirrels make nests under rocks or in ground burrows and live in social colonies in grasslands, shrublands, open woodlands, or rocky areas from prairie to alpine elevations. These omnivores feed on carrion as well as vegetation and are active by day.

68

Track Pattern: Living off fat and stored food, ground squirrels hibernate in northern areas from summer or early fall to late winter or late spring depending on species, latitude, sex, and age. Their four-print jumping track pattern with diagonally placed front feet (*upper a*) sometimes merges to two- or three- print patterns (*lower a*) and is common only in spring. The largest ground squirrels have tracks larger than those shown here, almost the size of prairie dog tracks.

Associated Signs: Ground squirrels are easy to see along with their tracks. Their sharp whistles and trilling calls are a sure sign of spring. Burrows (2 to over 3 inches wide) often have dirt and scats near openings.

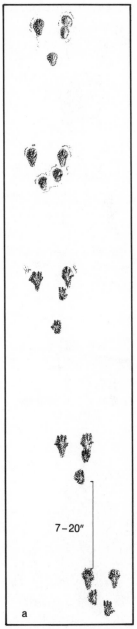

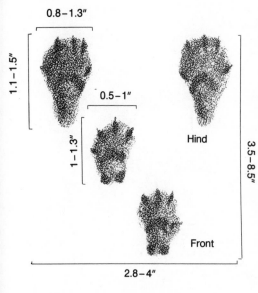

0.8–1.3"

1.1–1.5"

0.5–1"

1–1.3"

Hind

Front

3.5–8.5"

7–20"

2.8–4"

a

69

PRAIRIE DOGS
Cynomys species

Description: These medium-sized squirrels are light brown in color and have short legs, hind feet larger than front feet, and short black or white-tipped tails. Total length is 12.5 to 16.5 inches with a tail 1.5 to 4.5 inches. Weight is 1.5 to 3 pounds.

Habits: Colonial plains dwellers and ground burrowers, prairie dogs are diurnal herbivores. Historically, they were widely poisoned because of their suspected competition with western livestock for forage. Open grass and shrublands are where you'll find their colonies or "towns." One species, the Utah prairie dog (*Cynomys parvidens*), is listed as endangered.

1"

Track Pattern: White-tailed prairie dog species hibernate from late summer or fall to February, March, or April, depending on location and age. Conversely, the black-tailed species only reduces its activity in winter. Track patterns vary from an ungainly four-print bound with diagonally placed front feet (*a*) to a waddling alternating walk, where they often drag their bodies and feet (*b*). They may also run in a four-print loping pattern (*c*). Their trails, often several along one route, run between burrows and feeding areas.

Associated Signs: Prairie dogs seldom wander far from their distinctive dirt-mounded burrows (openings 3 to 6 inches wide, sometimes enlarged by badgers to 10 inches or more.) Scats are commonly found near burrows, as are the occupants, lazily basking in the sun or standing to call a colony alarm.

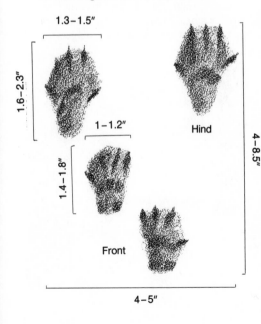

1.3–1.5"

1.6–2.3"

1–1.2"

Hind

1.4–1.8"

Front

4–5"

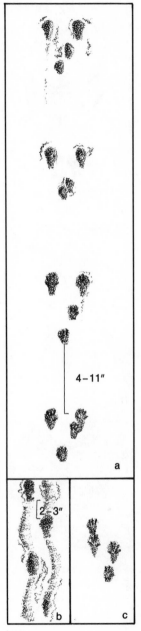

4–11"

4–8.5"

a

2–3"

b

c

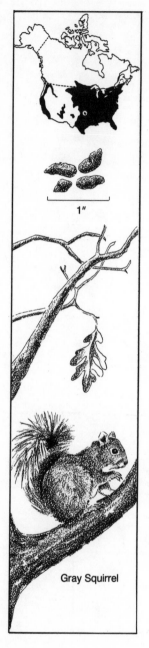

1"

Gray Squirrel

LARGE TREE SQUIRRELS
Sciurus species

Description: This group contains gray squirrels (*Sciurus carolinensis*, colored gray or black); fox squirrels (*S. niger*; red, gray, or black); western gray squirrels (*S. griseus*, gray); and tassle-eared squirrels (*S. aberti*, gray with red dorsal stripe). Total length is 17 to 27 inches with bushy tails 8 to 13 inches. Weight is 0.8 to 3 pounds.

Habits: Gray squirrels live in deciduous forests, fox squirrels in open forests or forest edges, western gray squirrels in oak and open conifer woodlands, and tassle-eared squirrels in open conifer forests. Gray and fox squirrels also live in cities. In fall, all but tassle-eared squirrels bury food for winter, mainly nuts, usually one item per cache. All are arboreal, diurnal, and somewhat solitary.

Track Pattern: These squirrels are active all winter and make a four-print hopping track pattern in which their front feet land side by side (*a*). The tracks may merge to form a two-print pattern when slowing down (*b*) or in deep snow (*c*). Squirrel trails typically run from one tree to another.

Associated Signs: Aside from spotting a scampering or chattering squirrel, you may find leafy nests on tree branches, although nests are usually in tree hollows, or excavated nut or seed stores. Like porcupines, squirrels gnaw on trees and saplings, but the damage and the tooth marks are usually smaller. Scats are occasionally found on snow.

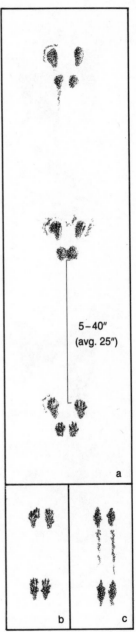

5–40"
(avg. 25")

a

b c

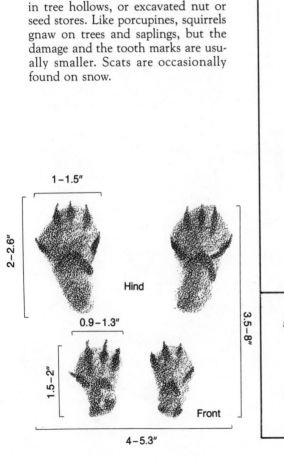

1–1.5"

2–2.6"

Hind

0.9–1.3"

1.5–2"

Front

3.5–8"

4–5.3"

73

Flying Squirrels

Red and Douglas' Squirrels

1"

SMALL TREE SQUIRRELS
Tamiasciurus and *Glaucomys* species

Description: This arboreal group includes red squirrels (*Tamiasciurus hudsonicus*, colored red-brown); Douglas' squirrels or chickarees (*T. douglasii*, dark-brown); and flying squirrels (*Glaucomys* species, brown or gray and white) with prominent fur-covered membranes along their sides. Total length is 9 to 15 inches; tail is 3 to 7 inches; weight is 2 to 9 ounces.

Habits: Red squirrels live in conifer or mixed forests, Douglas' squirrels in dense conifer forests, and flying squirrels in deciduous and conifer forests. The diurnal and solitary *Tamiasciurus* species store large conifer seed caches on the ground for winter, while the more social, nocturnal flying squirrels may store nuts and seeds in tree holes.

74

Track Pattern: Squirrels in this group hop making a squarish four-print track pattern with their front feet landing side by side (*a*). Front prints may merge (*b*). In deeper snow, hind and front prints merge into a two-print pattern showing foot drag marks (*c*). Flying squirrels seldom glide to the ground, but when they land, they may make a sitzmark showing their outstretched winglike membranes. Trails run between trees. All these squirrels den up in stormy weather, but only flying squirrels become torpid for short periods.

Associated Signs: *Tamiasciurus* species scold intruders with loud chattering. They tunnel through snow to nests and food caches near which may be found piles of castoff cone scales and cores (middens) and some scats. They also make leafy tree nests. Flying squirrels leave few signs, maybe a few gnawed nuts below their tree cavity nests.

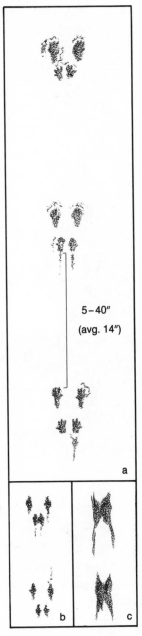

5–40"
(avg. 14")

a

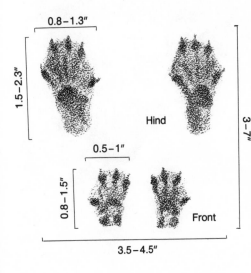

0.8–1.3"

1.5–2.3"

Hind

0.5–1"

0.8–1.5"

Front

3.5–4.5"

3–7"

b

c

KANGAROO RATS
Dipodomys species

Description: Tan above and white below with long tails and large hind feet, kangaroo rats are not commonly associated with snow country; however, one species, *Dipodomys ordii*, ranges into southern Canada. Its total length is 8 to 13.5 inches and includes a 4- to 8-inch-long tail. Weight is 1.5 to 2.5 ounces.

Habits: Kangaroo rats live in arid to semiarid regions with sparse shrubs or grasses and soft or sandy soil into which they dig burrows. They eat mainly seeds, which they store in winter, and are nocturnal, terrestrial, and solitary.

0.5"

Track Pattern: In winter, kangaroo rats travel on snow during warm weather but stay below ground for extended periods in severe weather. Like kangaroos, they hop on their hind feet when traveling long distances or moving quickly (*a*). Otherwise, they make a four-print hopping pattern with diagonally placed front feet (*upper a*). Their two-footed leaping prowess is impressive—several feet at a bound! Their trails run from burrows to feeding areas and often include tail drag marks.

Associated Signs: Look for the "K" rat's large, mounded burrows (entrances 4 to 5 inches wide) in the sand. Inside these burrows, it nests and stores seeds and root sections. Scats may be found near burrows.

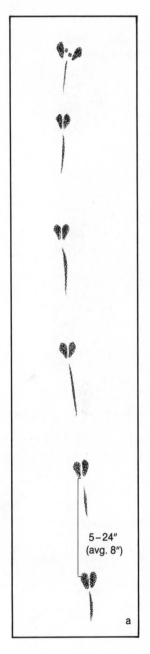

0.5–0.8"

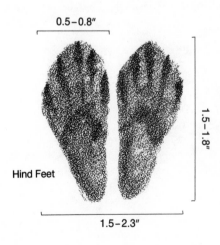

1.5–1.8"

5–24"
(avg. 8")

Hind Feet

1.5–2.3"

a

77

BEAVER
Castor canadensis

Description: Beavers, the largest North American rodents, are dark-brown with long, flat, scaly tails; short legs; and large, webbed hind feet. Total length averages 39 inches, the tail 18 inches. Weight is 30 to 60 pounds.

Habits: Mainly nocturnal and crepuscular, these semiaquatic rodents are restricted to slow-flowing streams and rivers or standing water where they feed on riparian trees, including aspens, willows, and alders, and other aquatic vegetation. They build winter caches of woody plants and live in small family colonies.

Track Pattern: Having winter stores, beavers restrict their land activity in winter but forage on land in

fall and spring. They walk in an alternating track pattern (*a*), which often shows large, webbed hind feet (and three or more long toes), and wide, snaking tail and body drag marks. Vegetation being carried may also drag. The hind feet may fall beside the front feet on hard snow (*lower a*).

Associated Signs: Beaver signs include dams of gnawed wood, domed lodges of wood and mud, beaver ponds behind dams, and gnawed trees and limbs on land nearby. Beavers stand on the ground to gnaw on trees, leaving broad teeth marks penetrating deep into the heartwood. (*Note:* "Ground" can be the top of a 4-foot-deep snowpack!) They are similar to but deeper and lower down on trees than porcupine gnawings. Scats are not deposited on land.

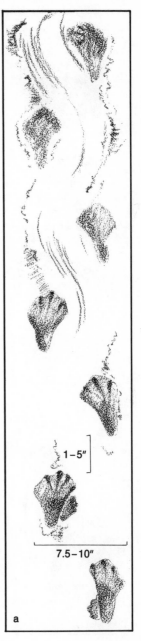

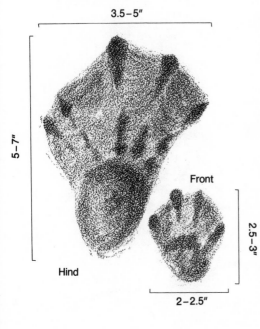

3.5–5"

5–7"

Front

Hind

2.5–3"

2–2.5"

1–5"

7.5–10"

a

79

MICE
Cricetidae and Muridae

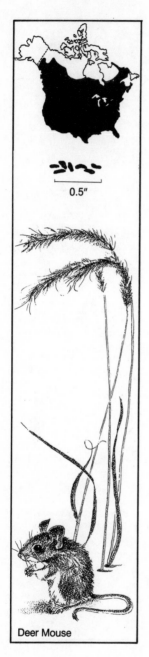

0.5"

Deer Mouse

Description: Most mice are dark above and light below and generally have long tails (naked for the introduced house mouse, *Mus musculus*), slender bodies, and relatively large hind feet. Total length ranges from 4 to 10 inches with tails from 1 to 6 inches. Weight is 0.2 to 1.4 ounces.

Habits: Most mouse species prefer grasslands, others rocky and brushy areas or wooded and semiwooded areas. Some are tolerant of human habitation, especially the house mouse. Most are gregarious seed eaters and semiarboreal, except the solitary, carnivorous grasshopper mice (*Onychomys* species). All are largely nocturnal and active year-round.

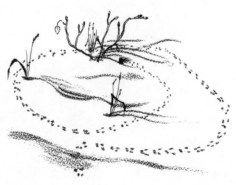

Track Pattern: Mice make a tiny four-print hopping track pattern (*upper a*). Their front feet usually land side-by-side, but sometimes they land diagonally for a few prints. One exception—James Halfpenny found that ground-dwelling grasshopper mice regularly place their front feet diagonally. In soft snow, the track often merges to a two-print pattern with a tail drag mark (*lower a*), resembling a small, linked chain. The relatively short intergroup distances help to avoid confusion with a vole's two-print track.

Associated Signs: You may trail a mouse to its burrow openings (1.5–1.8″ wide) in snow or to natural entryways leading under the snowpack. There, they share subnivean runways made by other small rodents. Small, dark scats are rarely seen on the snow, but more often in an invaded cabin.

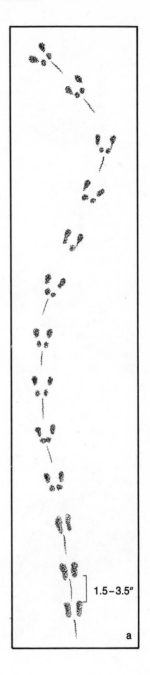

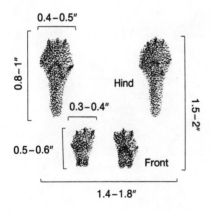

81

WOODRATS
Neotoma species

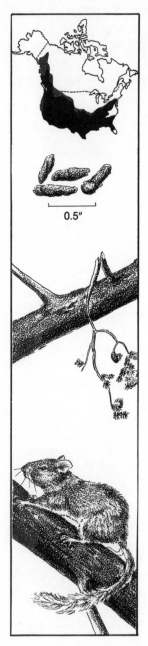

0.5"

Description: Woodrats, alias pack rats, have long, fur-covered tails, gray to brown pelage, and hind feet larger than front feet. Total length ranges from 11 to 19 inches with a tail 3 to 9 inches long. They weigh 7 to 20 ounces.

Habits: Solitary and nocturnal, woodrats prefer rugged, rocky terrain in woodlands or shrublands where they make large, bulky nests and feed on nearby vegetation. The name "pack rat" derives from the woodrat habit of trading dull nest materials they happen to be carrying for brighter, more attractive ones (e.g., jewelry, small utensils, garbage).

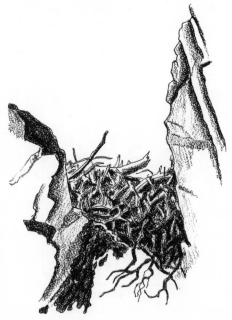

Track Pattern: Woodrats are active year-round, although they restrict their activity in severe weather. They usually hop in a four-print track pattern with diagonally placed front feet (*lower a*), similar to that of the chipmunk and rat. Their tails drag in soft snow. They may also walk in an alternating pattern (*upper a*) and tunnel under the snow. Woodrat trails are sometimes seen near rural hay stacks and backyards.

Associated Signs: Woodrats make conspicuous nests—elaborate piles of twigs, foliage, bones, rocks, feathers, dung, or garbage, often added to by subsequent generations. Below those nests located on rock ledges or crevices, you sometimes see a rank, slimy accumulation of urine and feces. Piles of dry scats are also found near nests.

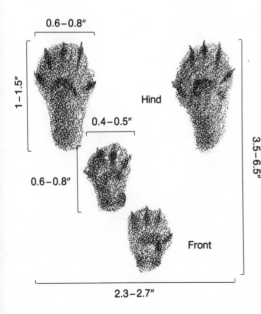

0.6–0.8"

1–1.5"

Hind

0.4–0.5"

0.6–0.8"

Front

2.3–2.7"

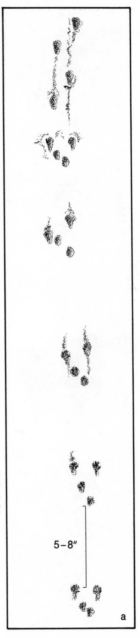

3.5–6.5"

5–8"

a

83

Lemmings

Voles

0.5"

VOLES AND LEMMINGS
Subfamily Microtinae

Description: Voles and lemmings are small rodents with chunky bodies, short tails, and hind feet larger than front feet. All are dull-colored, except for collared lemmings (*Dicrostonyx* species), the only rodents which turn white in winter. Total length is 4 to 10 inches with the tail 0.5 to 3.5 inches. Weight is 0.5 to 6 ounces.

Habits: Often colonial, these mostly terrestrial herbivores prefer moist habitats in woodlands, grasslands, brush, and tundra, although some species prefer drier areas. One species is semi-aquatic. They may be active any time during the year, day or night, and they huddle together in nests for warmth when resting.

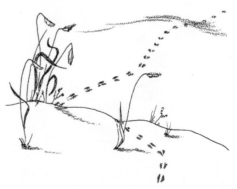

Track Pattern: Voles (*Phenacomys, Microtus, Clethrionomys,* and *Lagurus* species) and bog lemmings (*Synaptomys* species) jump making a four-print pattern with diagonally placed front feet (unlike mice) (*b*). This often merges to a two-print pattern for voles (*upper a*). In soft snow, feet drag, but tails drag only rarely (unlike mice). The gait may slow periodically to a walk (maybe scurrying trot) in an alternating pattern (*lower a*). Like voles, lemmings (*Lemmus* and *Dicrostonyx* species) walk in snow but may also make a four-print loping track pattern (*c*).

Associated Signs: Look for vole and lemming trails leading under snow to nests and feeding areas amidst subnivean tunnels and runways. Spring snow melt exposes grassy, globular nests, scat piles, and extensive litter-lined runways, vestiges of a busy winter world under the snow.

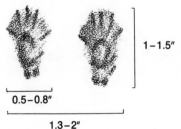

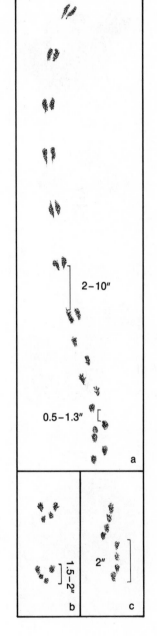

85

MUSKRAT
Ondatra zibethicus

1"

Description: Muskrats are red-brown with long, laterally compressed, mostly hairless tails, well-developed for swimming. Hind feet are larger than front feet. Total length is 16 to 25 inches with the tail 7 to 12 inches. They weight 2 to 4 pounds.

Habits: Another semiaquatic rodent, the muskrat is neighbor to the beaver, living in marshes, swamps, and along streams, rivers and lakes—ideally where water doesn't freeze to the bottom in winter. In winter, muskrat families remain active, feeding on submerged aquatic plants.

Muskrat House

86

Track Pattern: In winter, muskrats stay in their houses or the water, rarely traveling on snow. When they do, they walk in an alternating track pattern with a thin, serpentine tail drag (*lower a*), which may be all you see in deep snow (*upper a*). At times, muskrats hop making a four-print pattern with diagonally placed front feet, usually on ice or light snow.

Associated Signs: In fall, muskrat families living near slow-moving water build large domed houses of aquatic plants. Sometimes they cache vegetation in smaller domes, or "push-ups," covering plunge hole access points in the ice. Muskrat signs also include small scat piles and scent stations on rocks or glimpses of silently streaming muskrats—seen far more often than their tracks in snow.

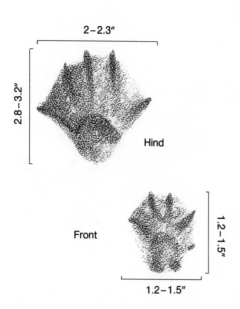

2–2.3"

2.8–3.2"

Hind

Front

1.2–1.5"

1.2–1.5"

2–4"

3–4"

a

RATS
Rattus species

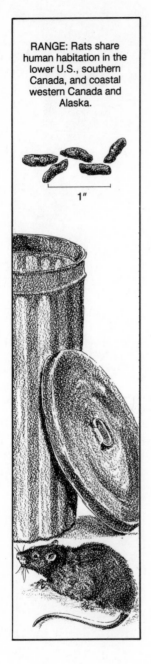

1"

Description: Rats arrived in North America with our founding fathers and are commonly associated with humans, particularly the Norway, or brown, rat (*Rattus norvegicus*). This brown to black rat has a long, naked tail and hind feet larger than the front feet. Total length is 12.5 to 18.5 inches with the tail 5 to 8.5 inches. Weight is 7½ to 10 ounces.

Habits: Rats are largely restricted to human habitats, especially cities, farms, and dumps, but Norway rats may also live ferally in extensive burrow systems in the ground. Rats are colonial, highly omnivorous, and active year-round, day or night.

Track Pattern: The rat track pattern is similar to that of the woodrat, a four-print hopping track pattern with diagonally placed front feet (*a*), except that you're most likely to find it in a city park, dump or farm grain storage area. Sometimes the track slows to an alternating walking pattern (*b*), or the four-print merges into a two-print pattern (*c*). Tails drag in soft snow.

Associated Signs: Rat trails may lead to small burrows (about 2″ wide) under tree roots and rocks, and scats may be found in a variety of places where rats and humans live. Destruction of food and fabric also signals the presence of a rat.

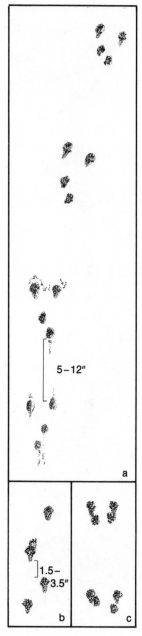

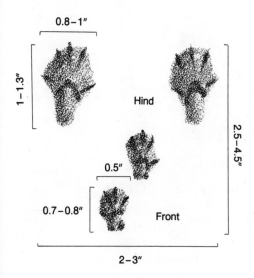

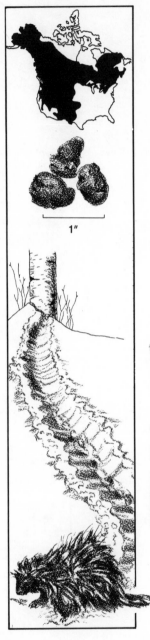

1"

PORCUPINE
Erethizon dorsatum

Description: Another well-known and widely distributed rodent, porcupines have dark fur interspersed with conspicuous long, stiff guard hairs or quills. They have short legs and wide, stocky bodies. Total length is 26 to 41 inches with the tail 6 to 12 inches. Weight is 10 to 28 pounds.

Habits: Porcupines prefer conifer forests, but they also live in a variety of other habitats, including tundra, desert, and mixed and deciduous forests—wherever they can find vegetation to eat. Their winter food is the cambium, phloem, and foliage of woody shrubs, saplings, and trees. Porcupines are solitary, nocturnal, and active year-around.

Track Pattern: Porcupines plod through the snow making a pigeon-toed alternating track pattern (*a*). It is similar to a badger's but has shorter intergroup lengths, quill drag marks and leads to trees rather than burrows. The hind foot overlaps the front foot in shallow snow. In soft snow, the porcupine's body plows a trough marked with foot dragging and the side-to-side swishing of stiff tail quills. Its trails run between dens and trees or brush, readily climbed for feeding.

Associated Signs: Look for porcupine gnawings resembling shallow beaver gnawings but high up in the trees. Scats are found by the bases of trees or at a porcupine's winter den—a cave or culvert or under a log or roots. A fresh trail usually means that Porky is nearby, resting in a den or tree or swaying uncertainly in a willow. Take a look around.

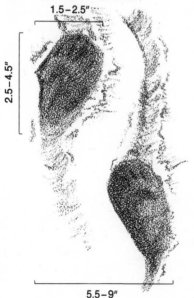

1.5–2.5"

2.5–4.5"

5.5–9"

1–8"

a

91

Carnivore Order: Carnivora

Most people hearing the word "carnivore" conjure up the image of a large, relentless killer tearing into some hapless prey. Although many carnivores (order Carnivora) are predatory, some are small opportunistic omnivores. (The term "carnivore" is sometimes confusing because of its dual meaning: any flesh-eating animal *or* any mammal in the order Carnivora.) All members of this order have large, conical canines and a specialized fourth upper premolar and first lower molar, known as carnassials or shearing blades. The terrestrial North American carnivores in this book are represented by five families: the dog (Canidae), bear (Ursidae), raccoon (Procyonidae), weasel or mustelid (Mustelidae), and cat (Felidae) families.

Carnivores are usually active when they are hungry. Some, like many mustelids, are more active at night, while others, such as bears, wolves, wolverines, and river otters, are commonly observed during the day. As a group they tend to be active in all seasons. However, where winters are severe, bears, badgers, and skunks build up fat reserves and remain inactive for extended periods. The bears' adaptations to winter are particularly complex: they are able to cease waste elimination and recycle their urinary nitrogen for months without a major reduction in metabolic rate. (Hibernating animals make this metabolic rate reduction.) Female bears also are able to give birth during this period.

Carnivores have a variety of social structures, some with complex social groups (wolves) and others using equally complex behaviors to remain solitary (many mustelids). A few, like skunks, river otters, and raccoons, live in small family groups when food is abundant. In some instances, female carnivores keep their young from the previous summer with them through the winter (lynx, wolves, bears), while other females do not (mustelids).

Carnivore food habits are also variable. Polar bears, dogs, weasels, and cats are probably the most carnivorous, but plant material is occasionally included in their diet. Skunks and raccoons are highly omnivorous and opportunistic. Being slow, they tend to run across food more often than they run it down. Therefore, different foods acquire a seasonal importance based on their availability.

DOGS

Each carnivore family has certain distinctive track characteristics. Most people are familiar with a domestic dog track, similar to that of a wild dog—elliptical in shape with four toe pads, claws, and a heel pad with one lobe in front and three lobes along the back. Not all of these features may register in snow, especially soft powder snow, but most of the toe pads, a hint of the heel pad, and at least the claw marks on the front two toes are usually apparent. (Even in old, windblown, or melted tracks no longer showing toe pads, claw marks are often visible if you kneel and look forward into the track.) This is because dogs are heavy in relation to their foot size and, except for some foxes, do not have fur-padded soles. Dogs usually walk or trot in the alternating track pattern, but they may move for short periods at other gaits. When confused, keep following the trail—a dog trail soon reverts to the alternating pattern. Dogs commonly drag their feet in soft and even shallow snow, which will help you distinguish their tracks from cat tracks.

To tell whether you are tracking a wild or domestic dog, think about where you are. If you are on a ski trail or near a house or farm, it is probably a domestic dog. The real clue is the behavior or nature of the trail. When a dog follows you in the woods, it often bounds away after something exciting, returning later to you or your call with rushing bounds. In contrast, a wild dog usually conserves its energy by walking or trotting deliberately along its way, making a narrow, regular trail. It may use man-made roads and trails (it *is* easier after all). Though sometimes playing, it seldom rushes around recklessly in the energy-demanding snow.

Distinguishing between wild dog species is sometimes a challenge, particularly between coyotes and foxes. But if you take several track measurements, especially of foot and straddle widths, you will obtain averages that will tell you who you're tracking.

BEARS

Bear tracks are unmistakable—they are large and look disturbingly human. When a bear walks in mud, sand, or shallow snow, its hind feet usually land ahead of its front-foot prints. In deep or soft snow, the hind foot registers on the front-foot print in a neat, alternating track pattern. A bear's front feet have small heel pads that often do not register in soft snow. Bears may also lope for short distances in one of the four-print galloping patterns.

MUSTELIDS

The mustelids, or weasel family, are named for their prominent scent glands, most magnificently developed in the skunk. They lope, making a characteristic two-print track pattern. The two prints are usually placed one slightly behind the other. Knowing this will help you distinguish tracks of small weasels from rodent tracks with a paired two-print pattern. The mustelid two-print is usually longer than wide, as are the tear-drop-shaped hind feet. Mustelids have five toe pads, claws, and a long heel pad on the hind foot. For most mustelids, these features are obscured in snow by the winter fur that grows on their soles. Except on very firm snow, only the claws of wolverines, badgers, and skunks are usually seen in tracks. Untypically, river otters have large, webbed hind feet.

The three smallest weasels almost exclusively use the two-print loping gait because for them this is the most energy-efficient way of moving through the snow. Curiously, they also tend to drag their feet and body between alternate leaps in deep snow (see the short-tailed weasel track illustration). Small weasels spend a lot of time under snow, which both conserves energy and places them close to their prey.

As mustelids increase in size, the need to lope in two-print fashion diminishes, until, with wolverines, walking (alternating track pattern) and galloping (three- and four-print track patterns) occur more often. In deep snow, however, the two-print lope is still common. The exceptions to the rule are badgers and skunks. Badgers typically walk in snow (alternating pattern), and skunks either walk (alternating pattern) or lope (four-print pattern), depending on snow depth. Finally, be aware that mustelid females are notably smaller than mustelid males. Thus, tracks of a female of a larger species may overlap in size with those of a male of a smaller species.

CATS

At first, a cat track looks similar to a dog track, but compare the tracks of a neighborhood domestic dog and cat. Beside being small, cat tracks are also very round, have four toe pads, a heel pad, and no apparent claws. Tracks of wild cats are often as wide or wider than they are long, while dog tracks are longer than they are wide. Sometimes cat tracks show the two lobes at the front of the heel pad, but only rarely do the three lobes at the rear of the heel pad (not shown on track illustrations) register in snow. Watch how a cat walks in snow—deliberately. It lifts its feet high and places them down daintily, apparently in haughty disdain of snow. Whether or not this is the case, wild cats walk the same way. (Studies in Yellowstone National Park by G. Koehler and M. Hornocker indicate that mountain lions avoid areas where snow depth exceeds about 20 inches.) Cats rarely drag their feet, although their hind legs may sink into snow making a "handle" at the back of their prints. Dog tracks may also have small handles, but foot drag marks often obscure them. Walking is the rule for cats, much more so than for dogs.

Cougars and lynx, although different in body size and weight, have similar-sized feet and overlap in other track measurements. Lynx feet, relatively large and heavily fur-soled, make great snowshoes. Consequently, their foot pads are more obscured than cougars' and their feet never sink as deeply into the snow. Bobcat tracks are similar in size to fox tracks, but the different cat and dog track characteristics make differentiation easy in most cases.

RACCOONS

Raccoons and ringtails in the raccoon family make tracks showing all or most of their five toes, a larger hind-foot than front-foot print, and heel pads, which are hairless for raccoons and lightly haired for ringtails. Their two tracks and trails differ considerably, however. Ringtails have round tracks resembling cat tracks, and their semi-retractile claws may or may not register. They walk in an alternating track pattern; raccoons often walk in a rather unusual two-print pattern. Raccoons make elliptical tracks showing long, finger-like toes, heel pads, and claws.

A *final tracking note:* From a distance, dog, cat, and deer walking trails look similar in deep snow. If you look down along the trail and draw an imaginary center line in the direction of travel, the line fits easily between the widely spaced ungulate prints on the left and right, but tends to intersect the prints of dogs or cats. The print itself often reveals whether the walker has foot pads, round or with claws, or has hoofs. Remember that cats rarely drag their feet, except in fresh, deep powder snow.

In the following illustrations, front feet are not detailed separately from hind feet for those carnivores that regularly place their hind feet in their front-foot prints. When this occurs, a slight increase in track size results, which is reflected in the measurements given.

COYOTE
Canis latrans

Description: About the size of a small collie, coyotes are gray-brown, often washed with lighter colors, and have long legs and tails. Total length is 42 to 53 inches with a bushy tail 12 to 16 inches. Adults weigh 20 to 50 pounds.

Habits: Still expanding their range across North America, coyotes typically live in areas of open prairie and desert, but are also found from forested mountains to alpine regions as well as in suburban areas. Primarily nocturnal, social at times, and active year-round, they feed on small mammals, carrion, various plants, insects and young of ungulates and livestock.

Track Pattern: Coyotes typically walk and trot in an alternating track pattern (*a*). The walking gait has shorter intergroup lengths and a wider straddle than the trot, and is used in deep snow. Less common gaits include a two-print trot (*b*) and a lope or gallop in one of the four-print gallop patterns (see *c* and Key on inside front cover). Coyotes drag their feet in soft or deep snow and their bodies in snow deeper than about 1 foot. Their oval tracks usually show foot pads and claw marks from at least the front two toes. Coyote trails may meander but are often bold, straight-line routes made by one or more individuals.

Associated Signs: A coyote trail often reveals a bounty of activities—a mouse chase, a roll in the snow, a meeting with other coyotes, scentmarks with urine or scats (doglike, often composed of hair or bone pieces), or a resting bed in the snow. Sometimes during the day you'll hear the "song dog's" riotous yips nearby.

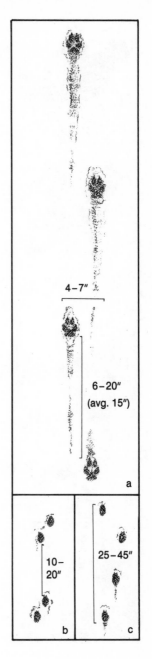

4–7″

6–20″
(avg. 15″)

a

10–20″

25–45″

b

c

2.5–3.5″

2–2.8″

2"

GRAY WOLF
Canis lupus

Description: Largest of the wild canids and the size of large domestic dogs, wolves are colored white to gray to black. They are larger and longer-legged than coyotes. Total length ranges from 55 to 82 inches with long, bushy tails from 14 to 20 inches. Weight is 70 to 120 pounds.

Habits: Wolf habitat, especially in winter, is intimately linked with the habitat of their large ungulate prey. This includes forests, arctic and alpine tundra, open plains, and arid areas. Historically wide-ranging but widely hunted, wolves are now restricted mainly to wilderness areas in the northern lake states, Canada, and Alaska. Social canids, wolves are active year-round, more often at night.

Track Pattern: Like coyotes, wolves usually trot or walk in an alternating pattern (*a*), but they sometimes trot in a two-print pattern (*b*) or lope in four-print galloping patterns in shallow snow (see *c* and Key on inside front cover). Wolves are more social than coyotes and may travel in packs of several animals, efficiently trailing each other or other mammals in deep snow. Wolf trails are usually straight and direct and often show foot drag marks. Their foot pads and claws usually register in the large, oval prints.

Associated Signs: Wolves urinate at scent markers and leave large dog-like scats almost completely composed of hair and fragments of bone or cartilage, mostly from large ungulates. Wolf howls are a distinctive long, low, rising monotone, and if you make one, wolves in the area might answer back.

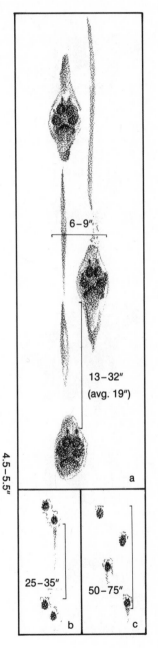

Arctic Fox

Red Fox

2"

LARGE-FOOTED FOXES
Alopex and *Vulpes* species

Description: Arctic foxes (*Alopex lagopus*) are white or "blue" in winter with thickly haired feet, while red foxes (*Vulpes vulpes*) do not change colors but have dark color phases. Both are the size of small domestic dogs with long legs and slim bodies. Total length is 32 to 45 inches with a bushy tail 11 to 17 inches. Weight is 7 to 15 pounds.

Habits: Arctic foxes live in arctic and alpine tundra and boreal forests, often trailing wolves and polar bears in winter to feed off their kills. They also catch lemmings and other small animals. Red foxes use various habitats including farmland but prefer semiopen areas in foothills and mountains. They eat small animals and carrion. Both are mainly nocturnal, largely solitary, and active all year.

Track Pattern: These foxes walk or trot in an alternating pattern (*a*) with their prints nearly in a line. In shallow snow, they may trot in a two-print pattern (*b*) or gallop in four-print patterns (see *c* and Key on inside front cover). Their dainty, oval tracks usually show foot pads, front claws, and foot drag marks. On firm snow, a transverse bar across the heel pad of the red fox may obscure the print of the pad. More wary travelers than wolves or coyotes, foxes tend to travel closer to cover. Arctic fox tracks are the larger of the two.

Associated Signs: Foxes urinate at scent markers and leave small doglike scats containing bone fragments or hair of prey. Look for spots where foxes have hunted small rodents by digging into the snow. Perhaps they left some blood and fur if they were lucky.

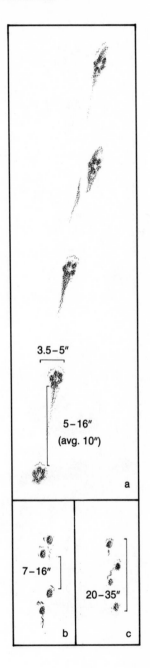

3.5–5"

5–16"
(avg. 10")

a

7–16"

b

20–35"

c

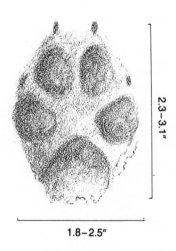

2.3–3.1"

1.8–2.5"

103

SMALL-FOOTED FOXES
Urocyon and *Vulpes* species

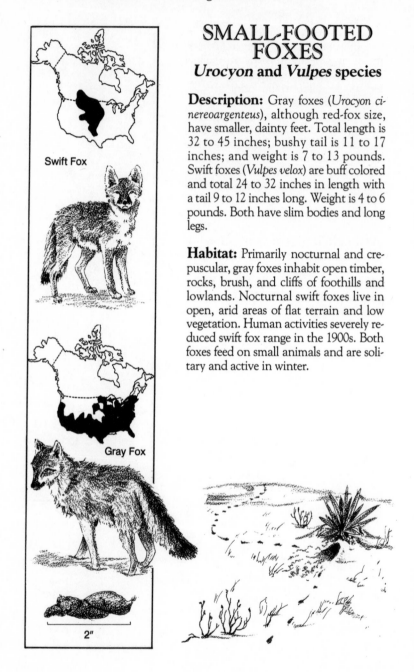

Swift Fox

Gray Fox

2"

Description: Gray foxes (*Urocyon cinereoargenteus*), although red-fox size, have smaller, dainty feet. Total length is 32 to 45 inches; bushy tail is 11 to 17 inches; and weight is 7 to 13 pounds. Swift foxes (*Vulpes velox*) are buff colored and total 24 to 32 inches in length with a tail 9 to 12 inches long. Weight is 4 to 6 pounds. Both have slim bodies and long legs.

Habitat: Primarily nocturnal and crepuscular, gray foxes inhabit open timber, rocks, brush, and cliffs of foothills and lowlands. Nocturnal swift foxes live in open, arid areas of flat terrain and low vegetation. Human activities severely reduced swift fox range in the 1900s. Both foxes feed on small animals and are solitary and active in winter.

104

Track Pattern: These foxes mainly walk or trot in an alternating pattern (*a*), but also break into two-print trotting (*b*) or four-print galloping gaits in shallow snow (see *c* and Key on inside front covers). Their oval feet drag in soft snow and parts of the small, dainty, doglike foot pads and front claws usually register (feet of swift foxes are slightly smaller). Gray foxes may climb trees, while swift foxes are the most subterranean of foxes, their trails sometimes disappearing down large burrows. Although they have small feet, gray foxes are large enough to have intergroup and straddle measurements in the red-fox range.

Associated Signs: Signs of this fox group include urinations at scent markers and small doglike scats that overlap in size with those of larger foxes. Following the trail of a swift fox may reveal the entrance to its dirt-mounded den (8 to 10 inches wide), often old badger holes. Gray foxes make less obvious dens in rocks, old trees, or brush piles.

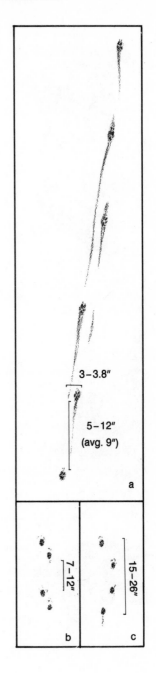

3–3.8″

5–12″
(avg. 9″)

a

7–12″

15–26″

b

c

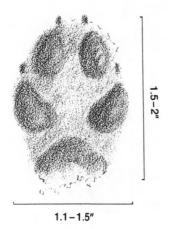

1.5–2″

1.1–1.5″

105

BLACK BEAR
Ursus americanus

3"

Description: Black bears are the smallest North American bears. They vary in color from black to dark-brown or cinnamon. Black bears have wide bodies and large feet with short claws (compared to a grizzly's). Total length averages 69 inches and tail 5 inches. Weight is 200–600 pounds.

Habits: Black bears live in various woodland habitats, as well as wet meadows and riparian areas. They are highly omnivorous, eating a varied diet that includes vegetable matter, small animals, carrion, ungulate calves, garbage, and, of course, honey. Mostly nocturnal and crepuscular, black bears are solitary except when with cubs.

Track Pattern: Black bears den in hollows, logs, rock crevices, or wind-thrown trees from October–December to March–April, depending on locale. In spring, they emerge and walk in a slightly pigeon-toed, alternating track pattern (*upper a*). The prints, with claws close to the toes, have an eerie resemblance to those of an unshod human. Watch for cub tracks in spring accompanying a sow, but give them a wide berth! In shallow snow, the long-padded hind feet often fall ahead of the short-padded front-foot prints when walking (*lower a*). A four-print lope may occur.

Associated Signs: Black bears climb trees, sometimes leaving long claw marks. They also stretch, rub and claw on "mark trees," perhaps to signal their size and presence to other bears. They overturn logs or rocks to hunt for roots and insects, leaving large, cylindrical scats composed mostly of vegetation.

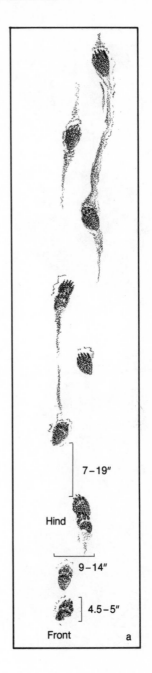

7–19"

Hind

9–14"

4.5–5"

Front   a

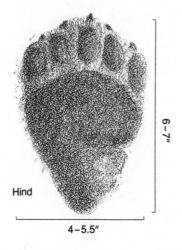

Hind

6–7"

4–5.5"

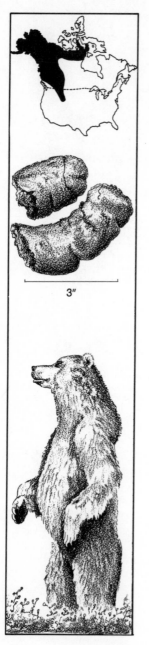

3"

GRIZZLY BEAR
Ursus arctos

Description: The grizzly bear group now includes the Alaskan brown bears. Grizzlies are blond to brown to black in color and have prominent, long claws on their front feet. Total length averages 75 to 96 inches with the tail about 7 inches. Weight is 400 to 1500 pounds.

Habitat: Grizzly bears are now restricted to open to semiopen areas in western mountains, arctic tundra, and the south Alaskan coast. Winter-killed ungulates and spring ungulate calves are important food for these bears when they emerge from their dens in spring, but normally they are surprisingly opportunistic and omnivorous. They are active day or night and are solitary except when with cubs.

Track Pattern: It's big! Sometimes emerging during mild spells, these bears sleep in high mountain caves, hollow or windthrown trees, or under rocks from October–November to March–April. They make an alternating pigeon-toed walking pattern (*a*) similar to the black bear's but larger and with longer front claws (extending 2 inches or more beyond the toe pads). In shallow snow, the hind feet overstep the front-foot prints (*b*). Grizzlies

may briefly lope in a four-print loping pattern. Tracks of bears south of Alaska are at the lower range of measurements shown, while Alaskan bear tracks are at the upper end.

Associated Signs: Grizzly bears claw, rub, and mark trees, but do not normally climb them. Their scats, similar to but larger than black-bear scats, have contents reflecting the current diet. You may see scattered conifer branches and shallow day beds around a den. A carcass covered by leaves and litter is the cache of a nearby bear—watch out!

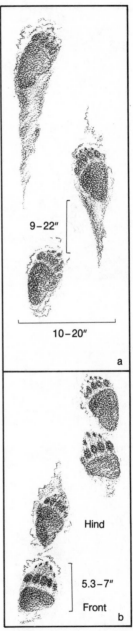

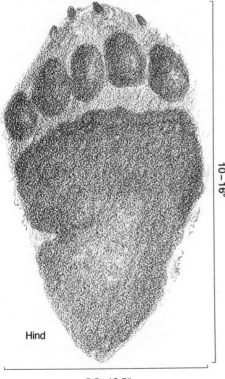

109

POLAR BEAR
Ursus maritimus

Description: This large white or pale yellow bear with only a black nose is ideally colored to blend into its arctic surroundings. Interestingly, the light fur does not reflect heat, but allows the dark skin underneath to absorb it. Total length ranges from 71 to 98 inches, and weight is 350 to 1500 pounds.

Habits: Polar bears range over the arctic ice and adjacent shores. These bears hunt mainly seals, snatching them by surprise at their breathing holes in the ice or in their snow lairs on the ice. These bears are excellent swimmers, active day or night, and solitary except in family groups. Hunting, now permissible only for Eskimos, severely reduced the polar bear population through the mid-1900s.

Track Pattern: Pregnant polar bears den in snowbanks or sides of ice pressure ridges from November to March–April,

110

emerging with cubs. Other bears den only temporarily to escape severe weather. Polar bear track patterns (*a*, *b*) are similar to those of large grizzly bears, but their short claws rarely register through their thick, fur soles. Polar bears often track each other; smaller bears to scavenge kills, larger ones to chase off smaller ones, and males to find estrous females in spring.

Associated Signs: Polar bear signs include large cylindrical scats (see grizzly scat) mostly composed of animal matter, and feeding areas, which are often visited in winter and spring by scavenging arctic foxes.

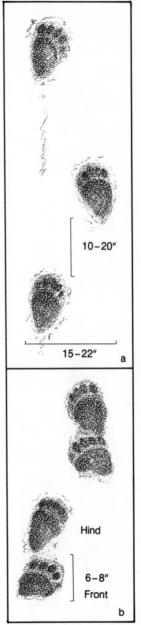

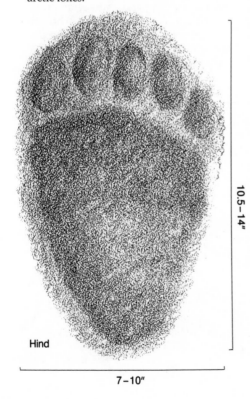

Hind

7–10"

RINGTAIL
Bassariscus astutus

Description: Ringtails are colored varying shades of buff with dark guard hairs. They have slim bodies, small, round feet, claws that may or may not be retracted, and long tails marked with prominent dark and light rings. Total length is 25 to 32 inches with the tail 13 to 17 inches. Weight is 2 to 2.5 pounds.

Habits: Depending on locale, ringtails prefer brushy areas among chapparal, rocky ridges, cliffs in the foothills, and sometimes forested mountains, often near water. Shy and partially arboreal, they den by day, often in pairs, in hollow trees, brush piles, cliff crevices, and un-inhabited buildings. They feed on small animals, plant material, and some carrion, and are active year-round. Ringtails are playful and tolerant of humans.

1"

Track Pattern: Ringtail tracks are different from those of their raccoon cousins—being much rounder, smaller, relatively shorter-toed, and somewhat catlike (but with an extra toe). Their claws are semiretractile and may or may not show up in tracks. Ringtails usually walk making an alternating track pattern (*a*), which may be slightly offset in shallow, packed, or wet snow. When ringtails travel, they keep to areas with adequate cover, so their trails are often hidden. In the higher, northern parts of their range, however, they do make tracks in snow.

Associated Signs: A ringtail trail may lead you to its den in the rocks or in tree hollows. You will only rarely find the ringtail's somewhat weasellike scats or see glimpses of this secretive animal.

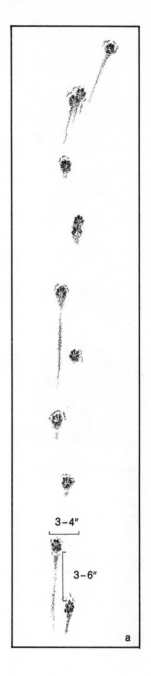

3–4"

3–6"

a

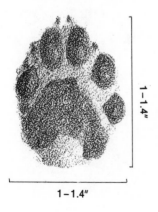

1–1.4"

1–1.4"

RACCOON
Procyon lotor

2"

Description: Masked and dark gray with a black-and-brown-striped bushy tail, raccoons have chunky bodies and relatively short legs with agile, long-toed feet. Total length is 24 to 38 inches with the tail 8 to 16 inches. Weight is 12 to 35 pounds.

Habits: Raccoons prefer brushy or wooded areas at lower elevations near water where they den in hollow trees, stumps, small caves, culverts, or abandoned burrows. Primarily nocturnal, they live alone or in small groups and feed on a variety of plant and animal material. They do not hesitate to visit garbage containers in suburban areas.

114

Track Pattern: In snow country, raccoons build up fat reserves and stay inactive in their dens from November–December to February–April to avoid both the cold weather and snow cover. In mild spells (around 20 °F) or in spring, they venture onto the snow, typically walking in an uncommon two-print pattern in which the hind feet fall next to the front-foot prints of the opposite side (*upper a*). At times, tracks in deep snow break into an alternating track pattern for short periods (*lower a*). Raccoons do not drag their tails in snow, although the long toes and claws often register. Their straddle increases in deep snow.

Associated Signs: Other raccoon signs are rare and include granular, black to brown scats of an irregularly cylindrical shape and omnivorous content. Of course, if a raccoon has raided your cabin or garbage, the mess is all too evident.

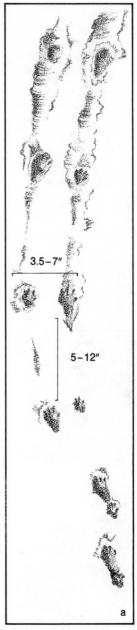

3.5–7″

5–12″

a

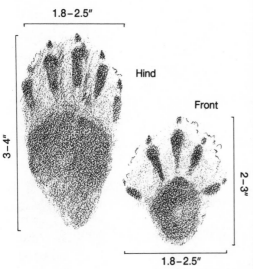

1.8–2.5″

Hind

Front

3–4″

2–3″

1.8–2.5″

115

AMERICAN MARTEN
Martes americana

1.5"

Description: This medium-sized mustelid has brown to rufous fur with a yellow to orange throat patch, short legs, and soles that are thickly furred in winter. Total length is 20 to 27 inches with the tail 6.5 to 9.5 inches. Weight is 1.5 to 2.8 pounds.

Habits: Primarily nocturnal and solitary, martens are restricted to conifer forests where they den in trees, tree cavities, or under the snow. They feed mainly on small rodents. Their range has been reduced in the U.S. and Canada due to overtrapping and habitat loss, although some reintroductions have been successful.

Track Pattern: Martens lope in an angled two-print track pattern (*a*). Their tracks may show claw marks and are large relative to other mustelids of similar body size. At times, martens slow to a walk (*b*) or speed up to a gallop (*c*). Their trails run through forests, across clearings, down holes in the snow, or to trees, which they readily climb. Martens often visit the subnivean world, resting in warm cavities under rocks, stumps, or logs, or hunting in the maze of runways and nests used by squirrels and small rodents. Tracks of male martens and female fishers may overlap in size.

Associated Signs: Tracks are often the only marten sign found in snow. Look for a rare scat or urination, or for sitzmarks with a tail print—a place where a marten landed after it jumped from a tree.

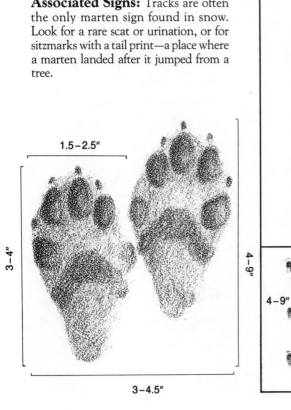

1.5–2.5″

3–4″

3–4.5″

8–40″
(avg. 19″)

a

4–9″

4–9″

b

20–30″

c

FISHER
Martes pennanti

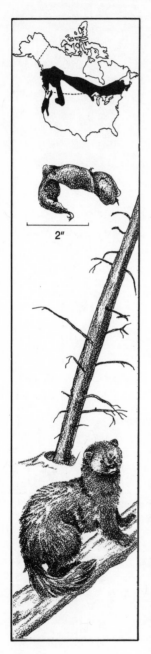

Description: The size of large house cats but with longer bodies and short legs, fishers are dark-brown but often gray in front and have thickly furred soles in winter. Total length is 33 to 41 inches; tail is 13 to 17 inches; and weight is 3 to 12 pounds.

Habits: Solitary, nocturnal, and active year-round, fishers live in mixed hardwood/conifer forests or conifer forests, at low to intermediate elevations. Over-trapping for furs reduced fisher populations in the U.S., but reintroductions have been successful, particularly in the east. Fishers den in trees or under rocks or logs and eat small to medium-sized animals, including hares, rodents, birds, carrion and, rather cleverly, porcupines.

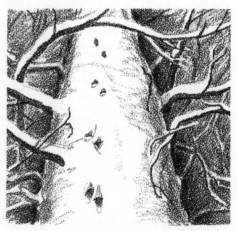

Track Pattern: Fishers lope in the angled mustelid two-print track pattern (*a*), similar to but slightly larger than that of martens. In shallow snow, fishers also walk in an alternating pattern (*b*) or break into a three or four-print gallop (*c*)—more often than do martens. Their trails run across clearings, through the woods, and sometimes to trees which are climbed. They enter the large subnivean spaces under logs and rocks to hunt and den.

Associated Signs: Other fisher signs include urinations and scats, which may contain porcupine quills or rabbit fur. These signs are rare, however, as is the inquisitive stare of a fisher gazing down at you from a dwarf mistletoe bundle or tree limb.

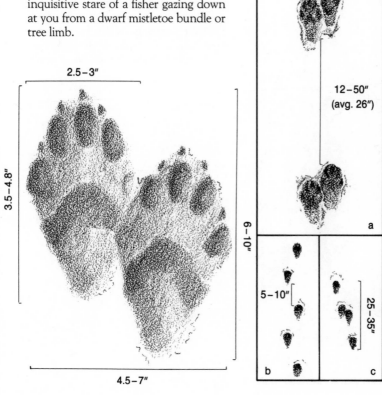

119

SHORT-TAILED WEASEL
Mustela erminea

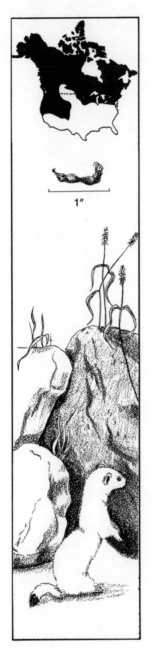

1"

Description: Also called ermines, short-tailed weasels are small weasels that turn white in winter except for the black tip of their tail. Total length is 8 to 14 inches with the tail 2 to 3 inches. Weight is 1 to 6 ounces.

Habits: Short-tailed weasels live in a variety of habitats, such as open meadows, stream bottoms, rock slides, tundra, and near forests—from sea level to 10,000 feet. They are more confined to mountains than the larger long-tailed weasels. Nocturnal and solitary, they feed on small mammals, especially mice and voles, which they cache in winter dens in logs, under roots or in burrows of small rodents.

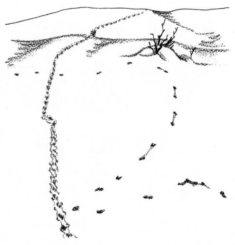

Track Pattern: Loping in a small, angled, two-print track pattern the size of fingertips touching snow, short-tailed weasels often alternate long and short leaps (*a*). Their bodies drag a trough between the short leaps in soft snow. Like other small weasels, their winter-furred feet rarely show distinct pads or claws. The energy and curiosity of this small carnivore is expressed in a trail that can cover meadows with wild zigzags, circles, double-backs, and short tunnels through the snow—the diligent hunting record of one ermine. Ermines often hunt under the snow.

Associated Signs: Look for tunnels in snow (about 2 inches wide) where ermines have hunted small rodents, and for rare urinations or scats along their trails. You may also see an odd trail with extra drag marks alongside. That's the trail of an ermine carrying prey in its mouth (see illustration).

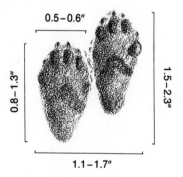

0.5–0.6"

0.8–1.3"

1.5–2.3"

1.1–1.7"

6–30"
(avg. 12")

a

121

LEAST WEASEL
Mustela nivalis

Description: The smallest of all mustelids and North American carnivores, least weasels turn white in winter but lack a black-tipped tail (but may have a few black hairs on the tip). Total length is 6.5 to 9 inches with the tail 1 to 2 inches. Weight is 1.3 to 2.3 ounces.

Habits: Nocturnal, solitary, and active all year, least weasels live in a variety of habitats, including meadows, fields, river banks, and open to semiwooded parklands and mixed forests, generally east of the Rockies. They feed mainly on mice and voles and often usurp the nest of a victim.

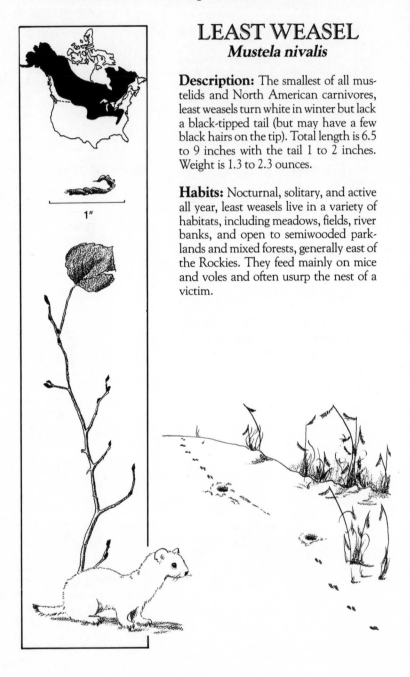

1"

122

Track Pattern: Least weasels lope making a tiny mustelid two-print track pattern (*a*). Measurements are slightly smaller than those of ermines, although the track pattern is similar. For general least weasel measurements, one friend says: "It's the ermine multiplied by 0.6!" Remember that measurements of a large least weasel male may overlap those of a small ermine female. Where the two occur together, the ermine is much more common.

Associated Signs: Least weasels, particularly females, spend more time under the snow than other mustelids—largely to survive cold temperatures, but also to hunt food. Sometimes they tunnel into snow to hunt for prey, making mouse-sized burrow openings (1.5–2 inches wide). They occasionally leave urinations and scats along their trails to mark their territories.

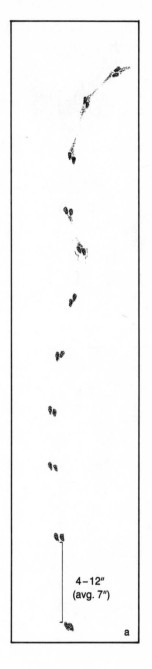

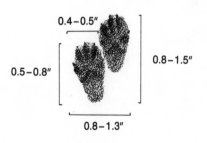

0.4–0.5"

0.5–0.8"

0.8–1.5"

0.8–1.3"

4–12"
(avg. 7")

a

LONG-TAILED WEASEL
Mustela frenata

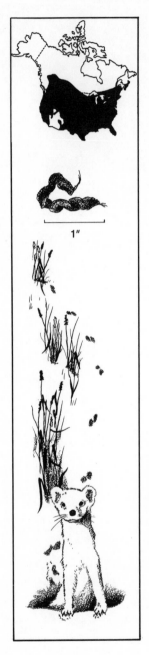

Description: Like other small weasels in northern areas, long-tailed weasels turn white in winter, except for a black-tipped tail. Total length is 12 to 22 inches with a tail 5 to 10 inches. They weigh 3 to 12 ounces.

Habits: Long-tailed weasels occupy a wide variety of habitats from sea level to alpine areas, including open grasslands, river bottoms, aspen parklands, woodlands, and alpine tundra. They prefer drier uplands of grass, forest, and rock and feed primarily on small mammals, especially voles and mice, which are sometimes cached in winter. They are solitary, mostly nocturnal, and active year-round.

124

Track Pattern: Long-tailed weasels make a typical mustelid two-print lope with their feet often at a slight angle to direction of travel (*a*). In soft snow, their bodies sometimes drag between alternate bounds. These weasels make straight or zigzag trails, and they dive under the snow to hunt for prey. Their tracks may overlap in size with those of large male ermines and small female mink and ferrets. But long-tailed weasels do not make the distinctly alternating long and short leaps of ermines, range farther from water than mink, and do not make large, diagnostic ferret diggings.

Associated Signs: Along long-tailed weasel trails, you may find scats, urinations, and burrow openings into the snow (about 3 inches wide). Occasionally, these weasels dig small piles of dirt out of rodent burrows.

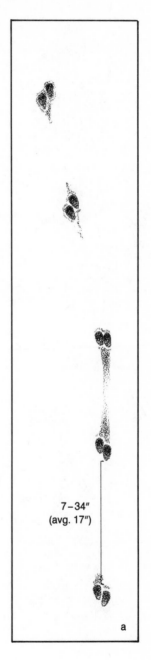

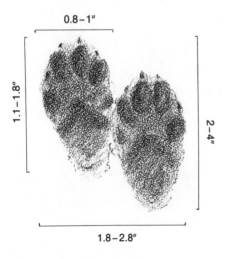

0.8–1"

1.1–1.8"

2–4"

1.8–2.8"

7–34"
(avg. 17")

a

BLACK-FOOTED FERRET
Mustela nigripes

Description: Black-footed ferrets have yellow-buff fur, a black mask across the eyes, black feet and tail tip, and a dark saddle. Total length ranges from 18 to 21 inches with the tail 2.4 to 2.9 inches. Weight is 2 to 2.5 pounds.

Habits: This endangered mustelid lives in close association with its major prey, prairie dogs, in whose burrows it lives. Brushlands and short-grass prairies are its home. Ferret populations declined precipitously after intense campaigns to poison prairie dogs earlier in this century. No wild populations are currently known, although ferrets may someday be reintroduced from captive populations. Ferrets are nocturnal, solitary, and active year-round.

Track Pattern: Ferrets lope making a typical mustelid two-print track pattern (*a*), which may slip to a three-print pattern (*b*). Sometimes, they slow to an alternating walk (*c*). Their tracks are similar to those of mink. However, ferret trails are associated with prairie dog burrows and ferret diggings, not usually with water.

Associated Signs: In winter, ferrets excavate dirt from prairie dog burrows, depositing it in long, thin piles that may have shallow troughs down the middle. These may be confused with badger diggings, but they are neater, rarely include large rocks, and often occur at burrows with openings less than 6 inches wide. Ferrets may also dig out a burrow and later drag their prairie dog prey to another burrow (see illustration), and they mark their territories with scats, urinations, and scent.

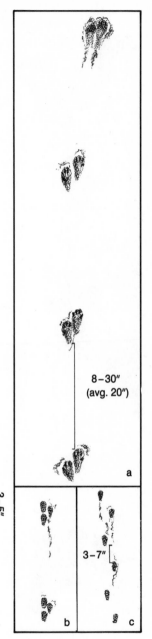

8–30"
(avg. 20")

a

3–7"

b   c

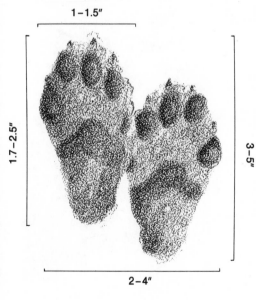

1–1.5"

1.7–2.5"

3–5"

2–4"

127

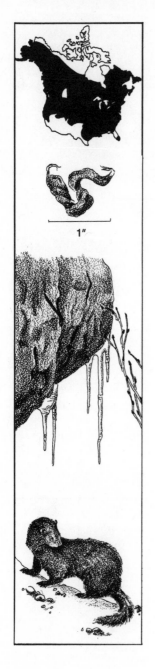

1"

MINK
Mustela vison

Description: This medium-sized dark-brown mustelid is shaped like other small weasels, long and thin with short legs. Total length is 18 to 29 inches with the tail 6 to 8 inches. Mink weigh 1.3 to 3 pounds.

Habits: Solitary, nocturnal, and active year-round, mink are semiaquatic and live near marshes, streams, rivers, lakes, ponds, forest edges, and tidal flats at a variety of elevations. They den near water under tree roots, piles of brush or logs or in muskrat or beaver dens in banks. They eat a variety of small animals, such as small mammals, fish, reptiles, amphibians, and birds.

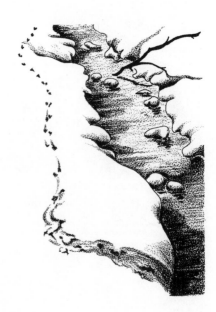

128

Track Pattern: Mink lope making an angled mustelid two-print track pattern (*a*), which may show three prints at times (*b*). They may also slow to a walk in an alternating pattern (*c*). In soft, deep snow, their feet, body, and tail may drag. Soles are not heavily furred in winter. Mink trails usually run along shores of waterways and often lead into the water.

Associated Signs: Like otters, mink seem to have a fun-loving nature and often slide through the snow into water, down embankments, or along level snow (often after exiting the water). These slide marks, 4–5 inches wide, are distinctly smaller than those of river otters (as are their tracks) but often occur in the same areas. Look for urinations and scats along mink trails. Scats are dark and weasel-shaped but often contain fish parts, fur, or feathers.

1.1–1.8″

1.7–2.5″

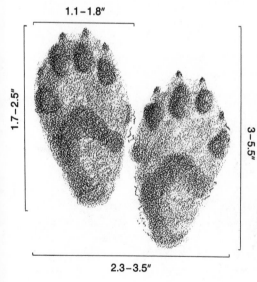

2.3–3.5″

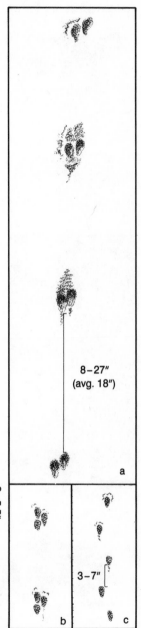

8–27″
(avg. 18″)

a

3–5.5″

3–7″

b

c

WOLVERINE
Gulo gulo

Description: The wolverine, the largest mustelid, is dark brown with broad, light stripes along its sides from head to tail. It has a stocky, almost bearlike body with relatively large feet and short legs. Total length is 32 to 45 inches with a tail 7 to 10 inches. Weight is 18 to 45 pounds.

Habits: Wolverines live in coniferous mountain forests and arctic and alpine tundra, now mostly in wilder, more remote areas. Solitary and active at any time year-round, wolverines are primarily scavengers, but also eat various small to medium-sized animals and sometimes ungulates—any of which they may cache for winter. They rest in the lee of rocks, trees, or slopes and may den under fallen trees, in rock crevices, or in snow.

4"

Track Pattern: This strong, hefty weasel has a variety of erratic gaits and nearly wolf-size tracks that usually show claw and foot drag marks. In light or firm snow, wolverines commonly lope in a three- or four-print pattern (*a*). They may also walk in an alternating track pattern (*b*) or resort to the mustelid two-print lope (*c*), usually in soft, deep snow. Even though their prints are similar in size to those of wolves, lynx and cougars, the wolverines' erratic gaits are diagnostic. Wolverines are wide-ranging and may cover many miles as they hunt for prey or search for carcasses to feed on.

Associated Signs: Wolverines leave urinations and large, weasel-like scats to mark their territories along trails. A wolverine's damage to traplines and cabins is legendary, but often overrated.

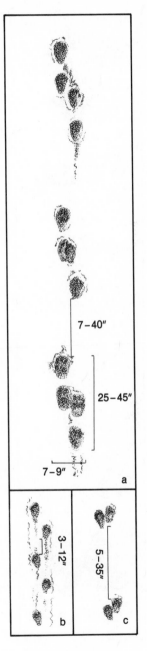

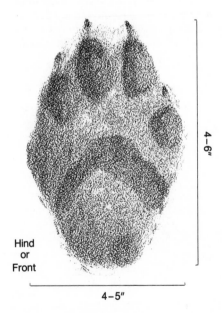

Hind
or
Front

4–6"

4–5"

7–40"

25–45"

7–9"

a

3–12"

5–35"

b

c

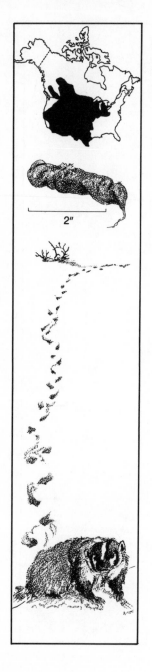

2"

BADGER
Taxidea taxus

Description: Built like small tanks with strong, short forelegs and clawed forefeet highly suited for digging, badgers are yellowish-gray with white-tipped guard hairs and white facial marks. Total length is 21 to 35 inches with a short tail 4 to 6 inches. Badgers weigh 13 to 25 pounds.

Habits: Badgers live in shrublands and grasslands as well as in the semi-open forests near them—wherever there are abundant ground squirrels, prairie dogs, pocket gophers, and other small animals to eat. Mainly nocturnal and solitary, badgers live in burrows they dig themselves or expand from rodent burrows.

Track Pattern: Unlike most other mustelids, badgers may den for several weeks or months in midwinter, depending on the severity of the winter.

Thus, their tracks are found in snow mostly in fall or spring. When badgers emerge onto snow, they walk, plodding in a pigeon-toed alternating track pattern (*a*) similar to that of the porcupine. However, badger trails lack the brushlike drag marks of quills, take longer steps, and are closely associated with burrows and diggings. A badger's long front-foot claws often register in snow.

Associated Signs: Badgers leave a large disorderly dirt pile when they dig out burrows hunting for rodents or making dens. Their burrow entrances are about 6 to 12 inches wide—the bane of many a horseback rider. Large rocks and dirt clods are also excavated, and fox- to coyote-sized scats and urinations are sometimes found nearby.

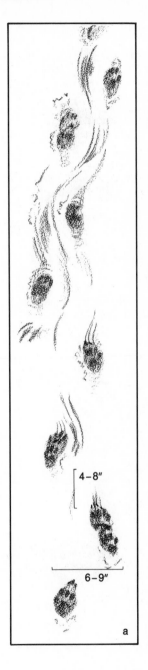

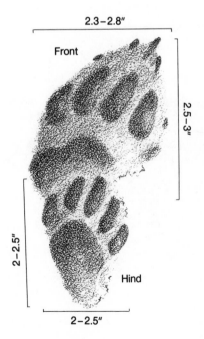

2.3–2.8"

Front

2.5–3"

2–2.5"

Hind

2–2.5"

4–8"

6–9"

a

SPOTTED SKUNKS
Spilogale species

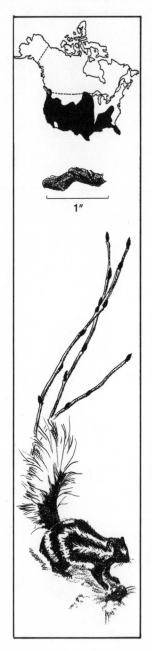

1"

Description: Spotted skunks are half the size of striped skunks and are colored similarly, except that their white stripes break into spotty patches along their sides and back. Their bodies are somewhat stocky with short legs and long, bushy tails. Total length is 11 to 24 inches with a tail 3 to 11 inches. Weight is 0.8 to 2.2 pounds.

Habits: Both the eastern (*Spilogale putorius*) and western (*S. gracilis*) spotted skunks live in scrubland, canyons, and farmlands. Primarily nocturnal, they eat a wide variety of small animals and plants, are moderately social, and den in abandoned burrows, brushpiles, logs or old buildings.

Track Pattern: These small skunks do not truly hibernate in winter but do den up in adverse weather, often with other family members. When they emerge on mild winter days, they usually walk or trot in a sometimes irregular alternating track pattern (*upper a*), or they may move in a four-print loping track pattern (*lower a*). Long claws on the front feet, well-suited for digging, often register in snow. Spotted skunk trails meander through the brush and may even lead to trees which these skunks will climb.

Associated Signs: Spotted skunks share the same unmistakable odor with their more common striped relatives. You may find places where a spotted skunk has dug into snow searching for food or, on rare occasions, their scats, chunky and roughly weasel-shaped.

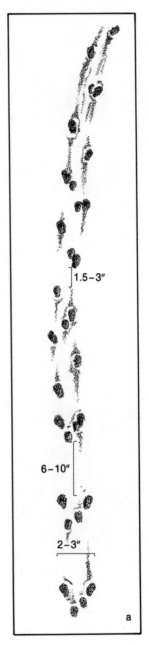

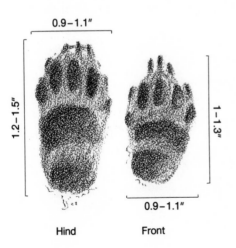

Hind   Front

135

2"

STRIPED SKUNK
Mephitis mephitis

Description: Striped skunks have short legs and stout, black bodies with two white stripes extending along their sides from head to tail. Bushy tails are carried high. Total length is 20 to 32 inches with the tail 7 to 16 inches. Weight is 6 to 14 pounds.

Habits: Striped skunks are widely distributed but prefer marshes, farmland, and riparian growth along streams in dry country. They do not generally occur at higher elevations in mountain regions. These skunks are more active at night than day; eat various small animals, plants, carrion and garbage; and den in usurped rodent burrows or under wood piles, cutbanks, stumps, or buildings.

Track Pattern: Striped skunks den up in cold weather, sometimes in small groups. When venturing outside, they vary their gait from a walk or trot in

a sometimes erratic alternating track pattern (*a*) to a clumsy lope in a four-print pattern (*b*), common in shallow snow. When loping, striped skunks make short leaps so that each four-print group falls close to the next, making it difficult to delineate one group from another. In deeper snow, skunks walk, their straddle widens, and their bodies drag. Foot dragging is common at most snow depths, and the long claws on the front feet often register.

Associated Signs: Skunks have developed the mustelid family scent glands into a fine and odiferous weapon. Often, the odor lingers in places that skunks have recently visited. Other striped skunk signs include digging spots and cylindrical, chunky scats, which are uncommon.

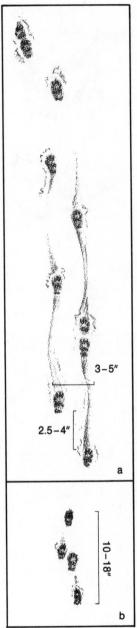

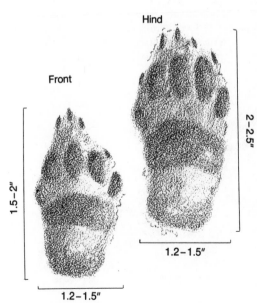

Front

Hind

1.5–2"

1.2–1.5"

2–2.5"

1.2–1.5"

3–5"

2.5–4"

a

10–18"

b

RIVER OTTER
Lutra canadensis

Description: This large and fun-loving mustelid has brown fur, large, webbed hind feet, and a long, thick tail well-adapted to life in the water. Total length ranges from 36 to 52 inches with the tail 12 to 20 inches. Weight is 10 to 25 pounds.

Habits: River otters are semi-aquatic and live in riparian habitats, such as lakeshores, streams, rivers, and ocean bays. There, they den in hollow stumps, under logs and roots, in beaver lodges, and in beaver and muskrat bank burrows. Active day or night, they often live in small groups and eat a variety of small animals, primarily fish.

Track Pattern: The trail of an otter is one of an exuberant puck unconcerned with meticulous foot placement. Thus, otter leaps, marked by large, webbed hind feet, form two- to four-print track patterns with accompanying tail flops (*a*). But why lope when you can slide? When moving, otters often drop on their bellies and slide, making troughs 8 to 9 inches wide and 40 inches or more long. Otters generally stay fairly close to water.

Associated Signs: No otter can resist a slide down a snow slope into the water, so well-worn hill slides 20 feet long or more are common. Along the shore nearby, look for resting and feeding areas with ample food remains, scats filled with fish parts, and urinations. The quiet visitor in otter territory is likely to see a bewhiskered otter face or two—or five—peering curiously from behind a snow bank or from icy water.

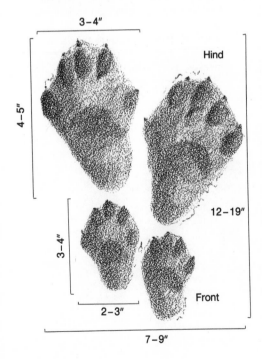

3–4"

Hind

4–5"

12–19"

3–4"

Front

2–3"

7–9"

13–21"

a

3"

MOUNTAIN LION
Felis concolor

Description: Mountain lions, also called pumas or cougars, are the largest North American cats. Colored gray to tawny, they have long legs and a long dark-tipped tail. Total length is 60 to 110 inches with the tail 21 to 31 inches. Weight is 80 to 200 pounds.

Habits: Mountain lions live in mountain forests and semiwooded areas from sea level to 10,000 feet wherever deer, their primary food, are abundant. They also eat small mammals, other ungulates, carrion, and livestock. They are mostly nocturnal, solitary, and active year-round, denning in rock shelters, caves, thickets, overhanging banks or hollow stumps.

Track Pattern: Mountain lions usually walk, making an alternating track pattern in snow (*a*). Sometimes, the

hind feet do not quite register on the front-foot prints in shallow snow. Infrequently, they gallop in a four-print pattern after prey. The heavy cougar's foot pads often register in snow, and their bellies drag in deep snow. Their round prints sometimes show lobes at the front (2) and back (3) of the heel pad on firm snow, but rarely show claws. Prints are as wide or wider than long. Their tails may leave marks at sitting spots. Trails are mostly straight and may lead to trees, which they climb.

Associated Signs: A cougar trail may lead you to a preferred, secluded spot where a kill was dragged and partially buried under snow or debris (also a bear habit in spring). Cougar scats usually contain fur and bone parts and resemble those of large dogs. Places where cougars have scented and urinated to mark their territories are found along trails.

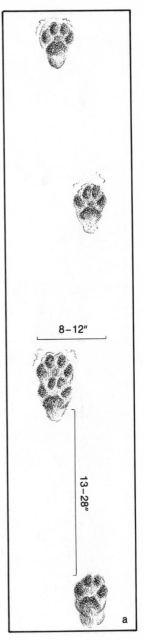

8–12″

13–28″

a

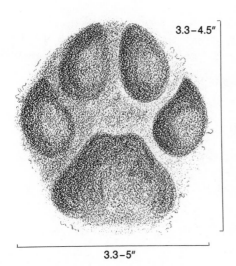

3.3–4.5″

3.3–5″

141

LYNX
Felis lynx

3"

Description: Lynx have mottled tawny, brown, black and white fur, long ear tufts, long legs, and a bob tail. Their feet, remarkably large and heavily furred below, aid in snow travel. Total length is 33 to 38 inches with the tail 4 to 5 inches. Weight is 15 to 30 pounds.

Habits: Mostly nocturnal and active year-round, lynx are solitary, except for family groups in winter. Lynx live in dense boreal forests but occasionally come out on tundra. They primarily eat snowshoe hares, but also take small mammals, some ungulates, and carrion. They usually rest in rough snow beds, either sheltered or in open areas.

Track Pattern: Lynx usually walk in an alternating pattern (*a*) and infrequently gallop in a four-print pattern. They place their feet "lightly" and deliberately, rarely dragging their feet or bodies. In deep snow, the hind legs sink, making a rear "handle" on the print. Lynx trails meander through the forest, unlike coyote or wolf trails, and may cross forest openings. The track pattern and print size are similar to those of the mountain lion; however, the straddle is generally smaller, foot pads are usually obscured by hair, and tracks sink no deeper than about 8 inches in the snow.

Associated Signs: Lynx leave frequent urination scent-posts marking their territories and scats similar to those of coyotes. They sometimes attempt to cover these and their kills. Resting beds appear as troughs in snow, deepening with use.

6–9"

12–28"

a

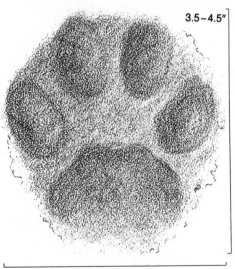

3.5–4.5"

3.5–4.8"

3"

BOBCAT
Felis rufus

Description: Bobcats have gray, buff, or reddish fur dappled with black spots, long legs, and a bob tail. Total length ranges from 26 to 50 inches with the tail 4 to 8 inches. Bobcats weigh 15 to 35 pounds.

Habits: Bobcats live in broken, semi-open and rocky areas in deserts and forests where they find shelter in rock crevices, under trees and stumps, and in logs and thickets. They feed on a variety of rodents, rabbits, and other small animals. They are active year-round, solitary, and primarily nocturnal. Bobcat populations have thrived with the habitat changes associated with humans, while lynx populations have declined.

Track Pattern: Like other felids, bobcats walk in an alternating track pattern (*a*), making prints about twice the size of a housecat's. They infrequently gallop in a four-print pattern. Their tracks, much smaller than lynx tracks, could be confused with coyote or fox tracks, but they have distinctive cat features—claws are rarely visible, prints are as wide or wider than long, and foot drag marks are rare. Like lynx, the hind legs sink in deep snow, making a "handle" at the back of the print. The toe pads are often visible; in firm, wet snow, the double-lobed front of the heel pad is evident. Bobcat trails meander rather than run directly.

Associated Signs: Along a bobcat trail, you may find urination scent-posts marking a territory and scats similar to those of lynx and coyotes. Bobcats tend to cover their scats, like housecats, leaving scratch marks in the snow.

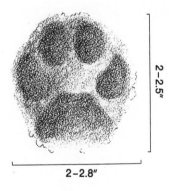

2–2.5"

2–2.8"

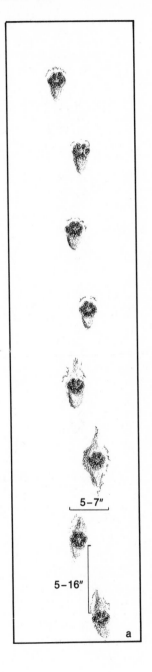

5–7"

5–16"

a

Even-toed Ungulates: Artiodactyla

The artiodactyls (order Artiodactyla) are even-toed ungulates and include three North American families, the deer (Cervidae), bovid (Bovidae), and antelope (Antilocapridae) families. Most walk on two-toed hoofs and have two additional reduced toes, dewclaws, hanging at the back of the leg above the hoof. These register in tracks only when the hoof sinks into snow a few inches. The other ungulate group, the perissodactyls (e.g., horses), walks on one toe.

Most artiodactyls are known for their exceptional running ability to elude predators, their efficiency at digesting herbaceous vegetation in a several-chambered stomach (involving cud-chewing), and their horns or antlers. Antlers, which male cervids (and female caribou) grow, are entirely bony. They are grown each fall, primarily for use in breeding behavior, and then shed each winter or spring. Male and female bovids and antilocaprids grow horns that have bony cores and keratinized horn sheaths. Bovids have unbranched horns that are never shed. Pronghorn (antelope) horn sheaths, branched on males, are shed annually.

Artiodactyls typically live in herds, except for moose, which are mostly solitary. Feeding either by day or at dawn or dusk, artiodactyls spend much of their time resting or bedded down, in contrast to the wide-ranging carnivores. Their beds are large, oval depressions in snow, usually crusted over from the animal's body warmth. Pieces of hair, distinguishable between species (and thus another tracking clue), are often iced into the beds. Artiodactyls also defecate frequently, leaving distinctive pellet groups by resting beds and feeding areas and along trails. (Droppings are always in pellet form in winter.) The stems of the dried or woody plants that they feed on in winter appear ripped or torn off, in contrast to the neatly clipped appearance of stems fed on by rodents. To uncover vegetation they paw away the snow, leaving distinctive "feeding craters."

Another habit common to many artiodactyls is migration to wintering areas. Some, like elk and caribou, move great distances to reach areas where winter food is more readily available. Others, like the deer, make shorter vertical migrations from highlands to sheltered valleys. In wintering areas where snow is deep, many artiodactyls stay relatively confined to areas (called "yards" for some deer) where they conserve energy by traveling on their packed trails between feeding and resting areas.

Artiodactyls typically walk, especially in deep snow, although they may also trot or gallop. When they walk or trot, they make neat (hind feet register on front-foot prints) or offset (hind feet fall close to but not directly onto front-foot prints) alternating track patterns. In shallow snow, an artiodactyl's walking pattern is often offset and the two-toed hoofs register clearly (the front is the pointed end!). In deep snow, their walking pattern is usually neat and resembles the walking pattern of large carnivores. However, an artiodactyl's straddle is usually wider and at least hints of the cloven hoofs and dewclaws are usually visible in the track. Also, artiodactyls commonly drag their feet, leaving two grooved troughs made by the hoofs. When frightened, artiodactyls may gallop in one of the four-print galloping patterns, except for mule deer that "stot"—or jump off all four feet simultaneously.

When distinguishing between artiodactyl species, look at the size and shape of the toes (all tend to splay in heavy snow), the straddle (it widens in deeper snow), the habitat, and the associated signs, especially pellets. In deep snow, the width of the slot made by the lower leg as it cuts through the uppermost layers of snow above the hoof print (usually narrower than the hoof) is often diagnostic.

Note: Because artiodactyls commonly place their hind feet in their front-foot prints, the front feet, slightly larger than the hind feet, are not detailed separately from the hind feet in the following illustrations. Measurements given reflect the size of the track resulting when the hind foot steps into the front-foot print.

ELK
Cervus elaphus

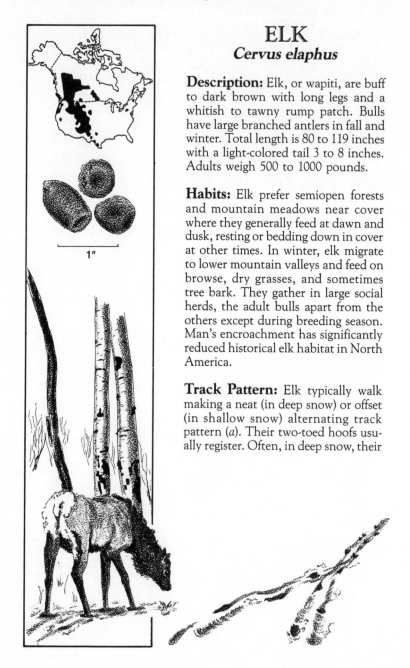

Description: Elk, or wapiti, are buff to dark brown with long legs and a whitish to tawny rump patch. Bulls have large branched antlers in fall and winter. Total length is 80 to 119 inches with a light-colored tail 3 to 8 inches. Adults weigh 500 to 1000 pounds.

Habits: Elk prefer semiopen forests and mountain meadows near cover where they generally feed at dawn and dusk, resting or bedding down in cover at other times. In winter, elk migrate to lower mountain valleys and feed on browse, dry grasses, and sometimes tree bark. They gather in large social herds, the adult bulls apart from the others except during breeding season. Man's encroachment has significantly reduced historical elk habitat in North America.

Track Pattern: Elk typically walk making a neat (in deep snow) or offset (in shallow snow) alternating track pattern (*a*). Their two-toed hoofs usually register. Often, in deep snow, their dewclaws register and their legs and feet drag, forming disorderly troughs between prints, the legs cutting a slot above the prints 2 to 3.5 inches wide. Often confused with those of moose, elk trails are narrower with more foot dragging and are commonly found in groups. Well-worn trails are made in wintering areas.

Associated Signs: Elk signs are common along trails and include nibbled and torn plants, ice-crusted, oval beds in snow, and elk hairs iced into beds. Also look for pawed out "feeding craters," pellets somewhat barrel-shaped and often dimpled at one end, and trees (particularly aspens) scarred by the elk's lower incisors, from feeding, or its antlers, from rubbing. In fall, you may hear the airy, whistlelike bugle of the bulls.

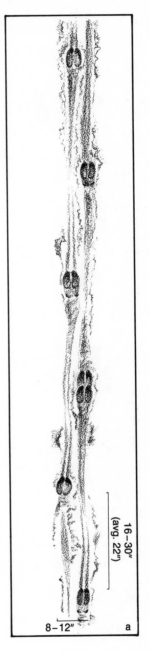

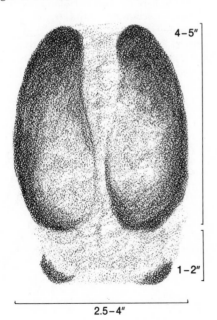

4–5"

1–2"

2.5–4"

8–12"

16–30" (avg. 22")

a

151

White-tailed Deer

Mule Deer

1"

DEER
Odocoileus species

Description: In winter, mule deer (*Odocoileus hemionus*) are dark gray with whitish rump patches and narrow, black or black-tipped tails. Antlers on bucks have two main branches. White-tailed deer (*O. virginianus*) are also gray with white rump patches, but they have broad, white tails and antlers rising from one stem. Total length is 46 to 82 inches with the tail 5 to 13 inches. Adult whitetails weigh 50 to 400 pounds, adult mule deer 100 to 450 pounds.

Habits: In winter, mule deer migrate from open western forests to lower south-facing hillsides and sagebrush steppe. White-tailed deer live in denser forests and brushlands (especially riparian ones), and in mountain country they migrate from hills to valley river bottoms in winter. Both species band or "yard up" in winter, browsing most often at dawn and dusk.

Track Pattern: Although mule deer are generally larger than whitetails, distinguishing between their tracks is nearly impossible. Check the habitat and range. Deer commonly walk in an alternating track pattern in snow (*a*). When galloping, whitetails make a four-print pattern (*b*) and mule deer jump stiff-legged, forming a four-print cluster (*c*). The small, sharply pointed, heart-shaped tracks are similar in size and shape to those of pronghorns, except narrower at the back. Foot dragging is not as common as with pronghorns. In deep snow, the dewclaws often register, the toes may spread apart, and their legs cut 1- to 2-inch-wide slots. Well-packed trails in deer yards run from beds to feeding areas.

Associated Signs: Deer signs are common along trails and include small, dark pellets, oval, ice-crusted beds in snow, deer hair in beds, and nibbled browse.

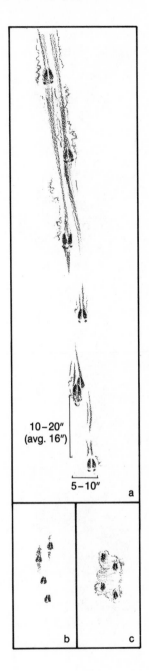

10–20″
(avg. 16″)

5–10″

a

b   c

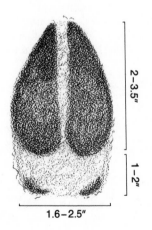

2–3.5″

1–2″

1.6–2.5″

1"

MOOSE
Alces alces

Description: Moose are large, dark-brown ungulates with particularly long, gray legs, high shoulders, and a broad muzzle. The bulls' antlers are broadly palmate and thick. Total length is over 100 inches and adults weigh 600 to 1600 pounds. Alaskan moose are the largest.

Habits: Moose prefer marshy (willow) areas in shrubby, mixed conifer/hardwood forests but also inhabit aspen parklands. In winter, they are often seen among riparian willows where they feed on browse and aquatic vegetation. Moose are usually solitary, but they may join one or two others in winter, sharing trails and feeding areas. Calves usually stay with mothers during their first winter. Moose are diurnal with activity peaks at dawn and dusk.

Track Pattern: Moose typically walk or trot in snow making an alternating neat or offset track pattern (*a*). Their two-toed hoofs usually register and make a slightly larger, more elliptical track than those of elk. When

Moose Bed

154

confused between the two, remember that a moose's legs cut wider slots in snow (4 to 4.5 inches wide), straddle is broader, and scats differ in size and shape. Also, a moose's dewclaws are often spaced far from the hoof in tracks. When moose drag their feet in deep snow (less often than elk), the drags form two parallel, continuous troughs that rarely show belly drag marks. Moose calf tracks are elk-size.

Associated Signs: Moose signs include ice-crusted beds in snow, nibbled and torn woody vegetation (particularly willows), tree bark scraped by their lower incisors when feeding, and long, dark moose hair. Their pellets, large and football-shaped, are particularly distinctive and commonly associated with moose trails and beds.

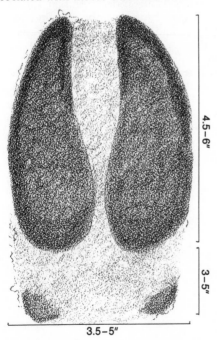

CARIBOU
Rangifer tarandus

Description: Caribou are light to dark brown with white throat fringes and rump patches. Both sexes have antlers that branch from a central stem with two palmate branches extending over the face. Total length is 50 to 101 inches, and weight ranges from 150 to 600 pounds.

Habits: Caribou live either in arctic tundra and open coniferous forests (barren ground caribou), or in boreal forests, muskegs, and alpine tundra (woodland caribou). In winter, some tundra herds migrate to forested winter ranges, while the woodland herds move down to lower forests. Both varieties are highly dependent on lichens for winter food. Caribou live in large herds and are more active by day than night.

Track Pattern: Caribou usually walk or trot in a neat or offset alternating track pattern (*a*) and often drag their feet. Their two-toed hoofs commonly register in snow, showing no-

Feeding Crater

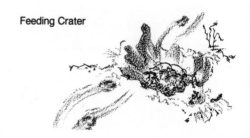

tably round, splayed prints with splayed dewclaws. These wide feet help serve as "snowshoes." Foot width and straddle approach moose size but prints are shorter and rounder. In deep snow, trails of both species show two parallel troughs from foot dragging, but caribou tend to swing their feet outward making the troughs slightly bowed. They make hard-packed trails between feeding sites. Other ungulates rarely share caribou winter range.

Associated Signs: Caribou signs include ice-crusted beds in snow, "feeding craters" pawed in snow to uncover lichens or vegetation, small trees rubbed by caribou antlers, caribou hair, and dimpled, elk-like pellets. Also look for spots where caribou pressed their noses near openings in the snowpack to smell for food.

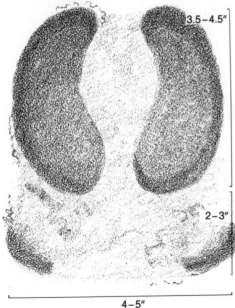

157

PRONGHORN
Antilocapra americana

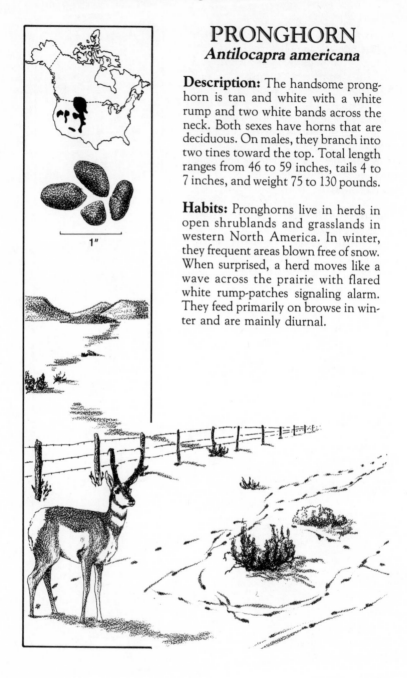

Description: The handsome pronghorn is tan and white with a white rump and two white bands across the neck. Both sexes have horns that are deciduous. On males, they branch into two tines toward the top. Total length ranges from 46 to 59 inches, tails 4 to 7 inches, and weight 75 to 130 pounds.

Habits: Pronghorns live in herds in open shrublands and grasslands in western North America. In winter, they frequent areas blown free of snow. When surprised, a herd moves like a wave across the prairie with flared white rump-patches signaling alarm. They feed primarily on browse in winter and are mainly diurnal.

1"

Track Pattern: Pronghorn trails meander among prairie shrubs forming a neat or offset alternating track pattern (*a*) when these ungulates walk or trot. The shape and measurements of pronghorn tracks are similar to those of deer but are wider at the back and narrower at the top. Pronghorns also tend to drag their feet more and do not have dewclaws. Where mule deer winter in pronghorn habitat, the two tracks are easily confused. When spooked, pronghorns gallop in a standard four-print pattern, distinguishable from the mule deer's jumping stot. If the tracks are fairly fresh, the herd itself probably won't be far away.

Associated Signs: Common pronghorn signs in snow include ice-crusted beds, urinations, small deerlike pellets, and pawed areas around shrubs exposing food. You may hear their flutey alarm whistles from the distance before realizing you're being watched.

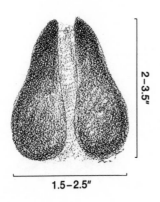

2–3.5"

1.5–2.5"

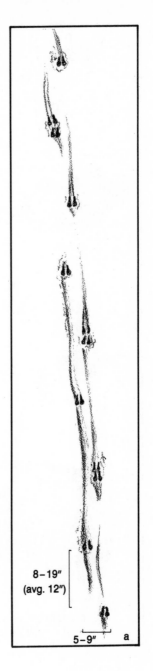

8–19"
(avg. 12")

5–9"   a

BISON
Bison bison

7"

Description: Almost everyone is familiar with the large, dark-brown bison or buffalo with its stocky body, large head, high shoulders, and woolly fur. Horns occur on both sexes and are short and upward-curving. Total length is 85 to 152 inches, with a 12- to 36-inch tail. Bison weigh 800 to 2200 pounds.

Habits: Historically, bison roamed prairie grasslands and shrublands in large herds, feeding during the day mainly on grasses but also on browse when grass was deeply covered by snow. They also lived in open wooded areas. Brought to the brink of extinction due to overhunting, bison herds have been reintroduced to protected areas in several western states and Canada.

Track Pattern: Bison tracks are two-toed, large, round, and similar to cattle tracks. Like other ungulates, bison walk in an alternating track pattern (*a*), often offset in shallow snow. They usually drag their feet between prints, and dewclaws register in tracks in deep snow. Where the leg makes a slot in the snow, it measures 4.5 to 5.5 inches. Bison commonly trail each other in snow, creating well-worn paths. Calf prints in spring are elk-size.

Associated Signs: Bison make cow-pie-looking droppings. However, you'll rarely confuse the two, because cows usually winter in fenced pastures and bison range only in known protected areas. Bison also leave swatches of unmistakable woolly hair. Instead of pawing the snow to expose vegetation, bison swing their heavy heads from side to side to plow a distinctive feeding crater.

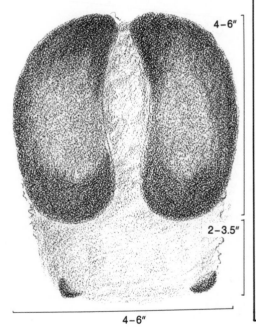

161

1"

MOUNTAIN GOAT
Oreamnos americanus

Description: Mountain goats have white to yellowish-white coats, and their stocky bodies have humps at the shoulders. Horns occur on both sexes and are short and backward-curving. Total length is 58 to 71 inches with the tail 6 to 8 inches. Weight is 100 to 300 pounds.

Habits: Surefooted keepers of the crags, mountain goats often perch precariously on or leap nimbly across rocky cliff faces. They are moderately gregarious, and in winter they often descend from their rocky cliff promontories to nearby forested areas or to slopes with a southern exposure. Their winter food is grass and browse. They are active during the day and parts of the night.

Track Pattern: Mountain goats walk in an alternating track pattern (*a*), sometimes offset in shallow snow. Their two-toed hoofs usually register in snow, and their long, narrow toes are often splayed. Foot drag marks are common and may show grooves where the toes dragged. Their tracks are similar to those of bighorn sheep but less inward-pointing and generally wider and more splayed; however, habitat is probably the most diagnostic clue. Mountain goat trails wind along rocky ledges, often leading up to prominent cliff edges.

Associated Signs: Mountain goat pellets, commonly found along trails, are small, round, and dark, and easily confused with those of deer and bighorn sheep. Again, observe the habitat. You may also find places where goats have nibbled mountain shrubs and twigs or bedded in snow.

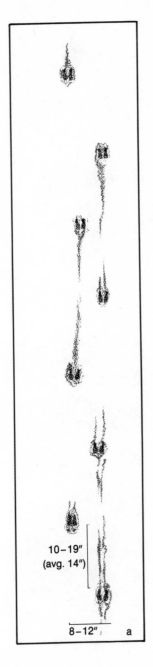

10–19"
(avg. 14")

8–12" a

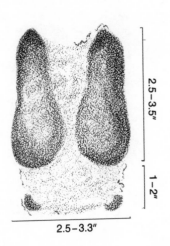

2.5–3.5"

1–2"

2.5–3.3"

MUSKOX
Ovibos moschatus

Description: A muskox is covered with long, coarse, dark-brown hair that reaches almost to the ground, so that the animal appears to be wearing a long, woolly skirt. Both sexes have horns that spread over the top and sides of their heads and then recurve outward. Males' horns are broader. Total length is 75 to 100 inches with a 3- to 4-inch tail. Muskox weigh 500 to 900 pounds.

Habits: Muskox live along the arctic coast in arctic tundra and feed on grasses, willows, and other plants. In winter, they move to slopes and hilltops where the vegetation is blown free of snow. They are mostly diurnal and occur singly or in small groups.

1"

Track Pattern: Muskox tracks show two-toed hoofs that are round and thick and similar to those of bison or cattle, although their straddle is generally narrower. In muskox range, however, it would be highly unlikely to find either bison or cattle. Muskox walk making an alternating track pattern (*a*). Their prints may be offset in shallow snow, the dewclaws rarely showing. Their feet often drag between tracks, and in soft, deep snow you may see marks where a muskox's long hair has dragged. Muskox trails wander through the tundra, where you may encounter a place where the band circled up to face a threatening predator.

Associated Signs: Other signs associated with muskox trails in snow include small, round pellets, urinations, patches pawed out in the snow to expose vegetation, ice-crusted beds, and long strands of muskox hair.

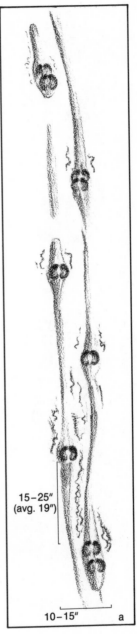

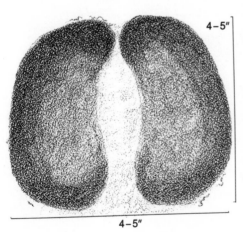

4–5"

4–5"

15–25"
(avg. 19")

10–15"   a

165

MOUNTAIN SHEEP
Ovis species

Description: Bighorn sheep (*Ovis canadensis*) are buff to gray-brown with whitish rumps. Dall sheep (*O. dalli*) are nearly all white in their northern range and gray-brown with a white rump in the south. Both species have horns: the rams' thick at the base and curling backward under the ear; the ewes' shorter and extending upward and backward. Total length is 47 to 78 inches with a tail 3 to 6 inches. Weight is 75 to 275 pounds.

Habits: The habitat of bighorn sheep, which once included prairies, is now restricted to open alpine areas in summer and lower mountain valleys in winter. Herds graze or browse by day and share winter range with elk and deer. Dall sheep move from high alpine slopes to lower south-facing slopes in winter, with habits similar to those of bighorn sheep.

Track Pattern: Tracks of wild sheep are squarish and similar in size to those of mountain goats (but not as splayed) and deer (but blockier and less pointed). They walk in a neat or offset alternating track pattern (*a*) with legs cutting a 2.5- to 3-inch-wide slot through deep snow. Their feet commonly drag even in shallow snow. Mountain sheep wintering together make well-packed trails used by herd members. Their tracks and signs are also similar to those of domestic sheep; however, in winter most domestic sheep are fenced in pastures away from mountain sheep range.

Associated Signs: Along trails used by wild sheep one finds small, roundish pellets similar to those of deer and mountain goats. These trails lead to ice-crusted beds in snow, which are often reused and littered with pellet groups and urinations. Look for places where sheep pawed away the snow to expose vegetation.

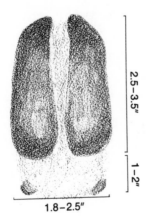

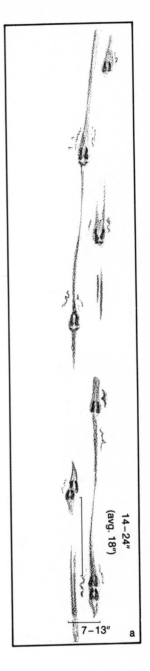

167

Some Other Track Makers

DOMESTIC ANIMALS

In winter you rarely find domestic animals in wild animal ranges, because they are usually fenced in winter pastures. Nevertheless, it is helpful for beginning trackers to examine domestic animal prints to better recognize those of their wild counterparts. It helps to practice taking and averaging measurements and to look at track variations caused by age, depth of snow, and animal weight. Dogs present the greatest potential for confusion with wild relatives, because they often accompany their masters on winter outings or may roam away from home.

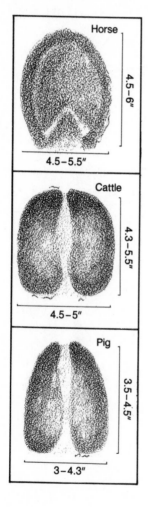

Horse

4.5–6"

4.5–5.5"

Cattle

4.3–5.5"

4.5–5"

Pig

3.5–4.5"

3–4.3"

Horse: Horse tracks are unlike any others because horses walk on one large toe. Mule and burro prints are similar but smaller. You often see the small triangular "frog" at the base of the foot and the outline of a metal shoe (more rare on mules or burros).

Cattle: Cattle tracks are similar to bison and muskox tracks; however, ranchers and farmers usually have cattle pastured in winter. Bison and muskox are sometimes pastured by private owners.

Pig: A pig print is similar in size to that of an elk, though not as round. There is little chance of confusion here—pigs are rarely far from a farmer's pasture.

Sheep: Domestic sheep have tracks and signs like those of wild sheep and are similar to those of goats and deer. In winter, you may find old domestic sheep droppings in a wind-blown spot and confuse them with those of wild sheep, thus requiring fresher evidence to prove it's wild sheep sign.

Goat: Domestic goats have tracks and signs similar to those of wild goats, but their ranges do not overlap, even in summer. Tracks and signs are similar to those of sheep and deer, but you are likely to confuse them only with those of neighboring domestic sheep in winter.

Dog: Domestic dog tracks are similar to wild dog tracks, large and small. When in doubt, check the animal's behavior and proximity to humans. A dog trail often shows exuberant leaps and bounds and association with human tracks. It is not the energy-efficient, direct trail of the wild dog, which does occasionally, however, take advantage of packed snow trails.

Cat: Most domestic cats choose not to take prolonged excursions in cold winter snow. It is helpful, however, for beginning trackers to examine the round, clawless domestic cat tracks and compare them to those of a neighborhood dog. An excellent lesson!

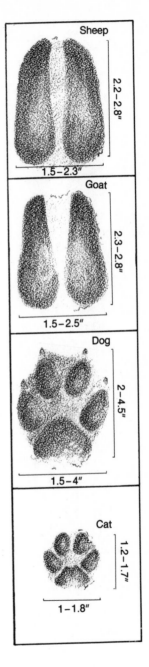

Sheep
2.2–2.8"
1.5–2.3"

Goat
2.3–2.8"
1.5–2.5"

Dog
2–4.5"
1.5–4"

Cat
1.2–1.7"
1–1.8"

BIRDS

Bird tracks in snow show three distinctive front toes, which may be somewhat obscured in soft snow. Their prints are often diamond-shaped making hopping or walking track patterns. Bird tracks may puzzle you at first, but follow the trail and it usually ends abruptly without a burrow or tree nearby and often with a wing-mark clue. Abbreviations used below are: intergroup length (INT) and straddle (STRAD).

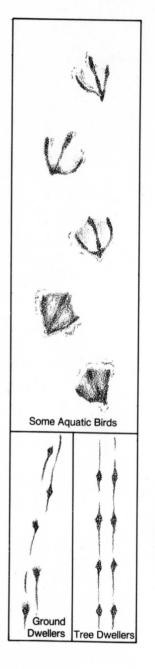

Some Aquatic Birds

Ground Dwellers | Tree Dwellers

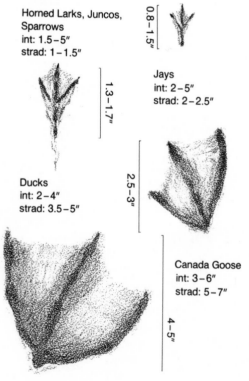

Horned Larks, Juncos, Sparrows
int: 1.5–5"
strad: 1–1.5"

0.8–1.5"

Jays
int: 2–5"
strad: 2–2.5"

1.3–1.7"

Ducks
int: 2–4"
strad: 3.5–5"

2.5–3"

Canada Goose
int: 3–6"
strad: 5–7"

4–5"

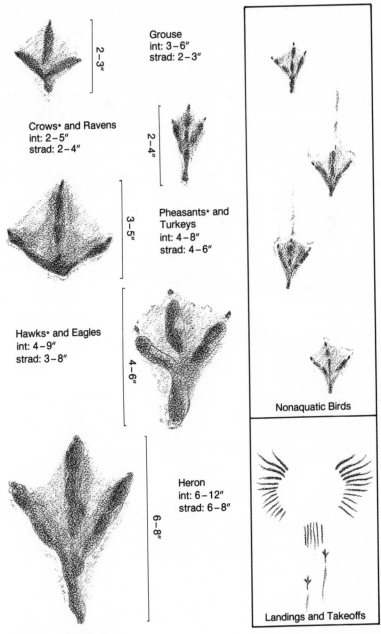

Grouse
int: 3–6″
strad: 2–3″

2–3″

Crows* and Ravens
int: 2–5″
strad: 2–4″

2–4″

Pheasants* and
Turkeys
int: 4–8″
strad: 4–6″

3–5″

Hawks* and Eagles
int: 4–9″
strad: 3–8″

4–6″

Heron
int: 6–12″
strad: 6–8″

6–8″

Nonaquatic Birds

Landings and Takeoffs

*Smaller track of the two

Glossary

Alpine. Of or pertaining to the area of elevated mountain slopes above timberline.

Alternating track pattern. A track pattern showing tracks spaced alternately along two parallel rows, typically made when animals walk or trot. Hind feet are placed on or close to front-foot tracks.

Arctic. Of or pertaining to areas from approximately latitude 65°N to the north pole.

Arboreal. Tree-dwelling.

Artiodactyl. A mammal in the order Artiodactyla having even-toed hoofs and including pigs, deer, elk, moose, caribou, pronghorn, goats, sheep, bison, muskox, and cattle.

Antilocaprid. A mammal in the family Antilocapridae, which has one member in North America, the pronghorn.

Antler. A bony outgrowth of the frontal bones of the cervid family; typically grown and shed annually by males.

Boreal. Northern; often seen as *boreal forest*, which refers to the coniferous forests growing in cold, dry climates with poor, sandy soil in areas including the Northern Hemisphere below the arctic tundra and high mountain regions.

Bovid. A mammal in the family Bovidae, which includes sheep, goats, bison, and cattle.

Browse. *n.* Woody plant material; especially shoots, twigs, and leaves of tree and shrub species. *v.* To feed on such plants.

Buck. An adult male of smaller cervids, such as deer and pronghorn, and of rabbits.

173

Bull. An adult male of larger ungulates, such as elk, moose, bison, cattle, as well as seals, elephants, and others.

Cache. *n.* A secure place for storing provisions, particularly winter food for animals. *v.* To make such stores.

Canid. A mammal in the family Canidae, the dog family.

Canine. 1. A dog or doglike animal. 2. A sharp, unicuspid tooth located in the upper and lower jaws immediately behind the incisors, typically with a prominent conical crown.

Carnassials. An upper premolar and lower molar in the jaw of mammals in the order Carnivora that fit against one another to create a shearing capability for tearing meat and cracking bones.

Carnivorous. Flesh-eating.

Carnivore. 1. Any flesh-eating animal. 2. A mammal belonging to the order Carnivora, regardless of its diet.

Carrion. The flesh of dead animals.

Cervid. A mammal in the family Cervidae, which includes deer, elk, moose, and caribou.

Colonial. Pertaining to animals living in a social group or colony often with an attachment to a discrete habitat or burrow system, as with colonial rodents.

Conifer. A cone-bearing plant, mostly evergreen trees and shrubs, in the order Coniferales.

Crepuscular. Active at early morning (dawn) and/or late evening (dusk).

Deciduous forests. Woodlands primarily composed of hardwood trees that shed their leaves at the end of the growing season.

Dewclaws. Nonfunctioning, degenerate toes on mammals that hang at the back of the foot and no longer reach to the ground.

Diastema. A space between consecutive teeth in a jaw, usually a result of evolutionary tooth loss or jaw bone elongation.

Diurnal. Active during the daylight hours.

Dorsal. Near or on the back.

Estrous. Being in heat, a time when females will accept a male for mating and are capable of conceiving.

Ewe. A female sheep, wild or domestic.

Family. A taxonomic category in the Linnaean system within an order and composed of one or more genera; names end in "-idae."

Feeding crater. A depression in the snow pawed out by the hoofs of ungulates when they expose plants to feed.

174

Felid. A mammal in the family Felidae, the cat family.

Form. A depression in the ground, vegetation or snow used as a place of rest and shelter; usually made by rabbits and hares.

Four-print track pattern. A track pattern showing four prints grouped together followed by a space and then four more prints, typically made by jumping rodents and rabbits, and by loping or galloping mammals. Hind feet are placed around and ahead of front-foot prints.

Genus. (pl. genera). A taxonomic category in the Linnaean system within a family and containing one or more species.

Gregarious. Tending to form social groups.

Guard hairs. Relatively coarse, long hairs that extend beyond and lie over the dense, insulating coat of fur.

Habitat. Type of ecological community where a plant or animal lives within its geographical range.

Herbivorous. Plant-eating.

Herbivore. An animal that feeds on plants.

Hibernate. To pass the winter in a state of torpor when the internal body temperature is reduced to bring physiological processes to a minimum; usually requires that animals prepare for it by building up excess fat reserves.

Horn. A bony projection from the skull covered by a sheath of keratin (the structural protein of hair and nails); typical of males and females in the bovid family and not shed except by pronghorn.

Intergroup distance. The distance between successive prints in the alternating track pattern or between print groups in the two- and four-print track patterns.

Insectivorous. Insect-eating.

Insectivore. 1. An animal that feeds on insects or more generally small arthropods and invertebrates. 2. Any mammal in the order Insectivora, including shrews and moles, regardless of diet.

Incisors. Simple teeth in the front tooth rows of most mammals that are well developed for chiseling and gnawing in rodents and rabbits.

Lagomorph. A mammal in the order Lagomorpha, including rabbits, hares, and pikas.

Lateral. Near or on the side.

Litter. 1. Offspring of an animal producing more than one young at birth. 2. The uppermost layer of organic matter on the forest floor.

Mammal. An animal in the class Mammalia that nourishes its young with milk from mammary glands and usually has the skin covered with hair or fur.

Mark trees. Trees that have been scratched by a bear's claws when the bear is standing up, possibly to signal its size as a warning to other bears.

Marsupial. An animal of the order Marsupialia, including opossums, that has a pouch where the young are suckled and carried.

Marsupium. A marsupial's abdominal pouch where the nipples are located and the young nurse and develop after birth.

Middens. Piles of discarded cone scales made by squirrels. Winter caches of cones are often located within or beneath the middens.

Mustelid. A mammal in the family Mustelidae, including martens, fishers, weasels, ferrets, badgers, skunks, otters, and wolverines, typically having well-developed scent glands.

Nocturnal. Active by night.

Omnivorous. Plant- or flesh-eating.

Omnivore. An animal that eats both plant and animal material.

Opportunistic. Using a variety of feeding strategies to eat a variety of foods whenever they become available.

Order. A taxonomic category in the Linnaean system within a class and containing one or more families.

Pelage. The coat of hair or fur on an animal.

Pellets. Roundish droppings of herbivores. During a single defecation, several to many pellets are deposited in a pellet group.

Prairie. A grassland; usually a naturally occuring grassland.

Premolars. Cheek teeth located between the canines (or incisors if canines are not present) and molars.

Push-ups. Domes of cached vegetation piled by muskrats over plunge hole entrances in the ice to provide food in winter.

Ram. A male sheep, wild or domestic.

Riparian. Pertaining to areas near natural waterways, e.g., around streams, rivers, and sometimes lakes.

Scat. A discrete piece of animal feces; droppings; the common term for carnivore feces.

Solitary. Single; referring to animals that do not gather in social groups but remain alone except when breeding or raising young.

Species. (pl. species). 1. The smallest taxonomic category in the Linnaean system within a genus. A species' scientific name is a binomial composed of two terms, first the name of its genus and then that of its species (e.g., the scientific name for coyote is *Canis latrans*, or *C. latrans* if the genus has already been mentioned, but not just *latrans*). 2. A group of animals that may interbreed but are reproductively isolated from other such groups.

Sitzmark. A depression left in snow after an animal jumps on snow, as from a tree; also where a skier has fallen.

Steppe. Semiarid grass and shrublands.

Stot. A movement made when an animal jumps off all four legs simultaneously.

Straddle. The distance between the outermost prints along the animal's trail; the width of the trail.

Subfamily. A taxonomic category in the Linnean system, a division of a family.

Subnivean. Pertaining to areas under the snow but above the ground.

Subterranean. Underground.

Terrestrial. Ground-dwelling.

Territory. A part of an animal's home range that is defended against other animals of the same species.

Torpid. Dormant; mostly incapable of motion or sensation, with a lowered body temperature.

Track pattern. A distinct arrangement of tracks made when an animal moves.

Two-print track pattern. A track pattern showing two tracks together followed by a space and then two more tracks, typically made by loping mustelids, walking raccoons and opossums, trotting dogs and ungulates, and small rodents jumping in deep, soft snow.

Tundra. A treeless ecological community in arctic or alpine areas that supports only low or dwarf woody vegetation and herbs. In arctic areas it is usually underlain by frozen soil or permafrost.

Ungulate. Hoofed mammal.

Ursid. A mammal in the family Ursidae, the bear family.

Yards. Areas, rather restricted in size, where some ungulates move, rest, and feed when snow is deep enough to make walking difficult. They conserve energy by keeping to well-packed trails.

References

Amstrup, S.C. 1986. *Polar bear.* Audubon Wildlife Report 1986: 791–804.

Armstrong, D.M. 1975. *Rocky Mountain mammals.* Rocky Mountain Nature Association, Inc., Estes Park, Co.

Banfield, A.W.F. 1974. *The mammals of Canada.* University of Toronto Press, Toronto.

Burt, W.H., and R.P. Grossenheider. 1976. *A field guide to the mammals.* Houghton, Mifflin Co., Boston.

Cowan, I. McT., and C.J. Guiguet. 1973. *The mammals of British Columbia.* British Columbia Provincial Museum, Victoria, Canada, Handbook #11.

Chapman, J.A., and G.A. Feldhamer, eds. 1982. *Wild mammals of North America: biology, management and economics.* Johns Hopkins University Press, Baltimore.

Doutt, J.K., C.A. Heppenstall, and J.E. Guilday. 1966. *Mammals of Pennsylvania.* Pennsylvania Game Commission, Harrisburg.

Gambaryan, P.P. 1974. *How mammals run: anatomical adaptations.* John Wiley and Sons, New York (translated from Russian Beg mlekopitayushchikh-prisposobitel'nye, Leningrad, 1972).

Godin, A.J. 1977. *Wild mammals of New England.* Johns Hopkins University Press, Baltimore.

References

Halfpenny, J. 1986. *A field guide to mammal tracking in western America*. Johnson Books, Boulder, Co.

Hall, E.R. 1981. *The mammals of North America*. John Wiley and Sons, N.Y.

Hazard, E.B. 1982. *The mammals of Minnesota*. University of Minnesota Press, Minneapolis.

Ingles, L.G. 1965. *Mammals of the Pacific states*. Stanford University Press, Calif.

Jones, J.J., D.C. Carter, H.H. Genoways, R.S. Hoffman, and D.W. Rice. 1982. *Revised checklist of North American mammals north of Mexico, 1982*. Occasional papers Museum of Texas Tech. Univ. 80: 1–22.

Kansas, J. 1984. "Tracking mammals in the Rocky Mountains." *Explore*. 14:38–44 and 15:31–35.

Larrison, E.J. 1976. *Mammals of the Northwest*. Seattle Audubon Society, Seattle.

Lechleitner, R.R. 1969. *Wild mammals of Colorado*. Pruett Publishing Co., Boulder, Co.

Murie, O.J. 1975. *A field guide to animal tracks*. Houghton Mifflin Co., Boston.

Muybridge, E. 1979. *Human and animal locomotion*, v. III. Dover, New York.

National Geographic Society. 1979. *Wild animals of North America*. NGS, Washington, D.C.

Nowak, R.M., and J.L. Paradiso. 1983. *Walker's mammals of the world*, 4th ed. Johns Hopkins University Press, Baltimore.

Pruitt, W.O., Jr. 1978. *Boreal ecology*. Camelot Press Ltd., Southhampton, England.

Stephenson, R.O. 1986. *Development of lynx population estimation techniques*. Alaska Department of Fish and Game, Final Report.

Stokes, D. 1976. *Guide to nature in winter; New England and north central North America*. Little Brown, N.Y.

Index

Index

Index

Gaspé (*Sorex gaspensis*), 39
masked (*Sorex cinereus*), 39
northern short-tailed (*Blarina brevicauda*), 40
Pacific water (*Sorex bendirii*), 39
pygmy (*Sorex hoyi*), 39, 40
water (*Sorex palustris*), 39, 40, 43
Shrew family (Soricidae), 39–43
Skunk, 19, 93, 94, 95, 96, 134–37
eastern spotted (*Spilogale putorius*), 134
striped (*Mephitis mephitis*), 136–37, 191
western spotted (*Spilogale gracilis*), 134
Slides, mink and otter, 129, 139
Snow, 14–16
adaptations for life in, 15–16
life under
carnivore, 15–16, 96, 117, 119, 121, 123, 125
rodent, 15, 16, 63, 75, 81, 83, 85
shrew, 15, 39–40, 43
Sparrow, 170
Squirrel
antelope, 59
ground, 24, 59, 60, 68–69, 187
tree, 20, 24, 59, 72–75
Douglas' (*Tamiasciurus douglasii*), 74
flying (*Glaucomys* species), 59, 74
fox (*Sciurus niger*), 72
gray (*Sciurus carolinensis*), 72, 186
large, 72–73
red (*Tamiasciurus hudsonicus*), 46, 74, 187, 190
small, 74–75
tassel-eared (*Sciurus aberti*), 72
western gray (*Sciurus griseus*), 72
Squirrel family (Sciuridae), 59

Tracks. *See also individual species.*
changes in size of, 25–26
deciding direction of, 29
identifying, 17–28
by habitat, 24

by shape, 25
by signs, 27–28
by using the key, 28–29
patterns of
alternating, 17–19, 21, 26, 33, 40, 60, 94, 95, 97, 148
four-print, 21–24, 40, 46, 60, 96
two-print, 19–21, 34, 40, 60, 95, 96, 97
preserving, 30
taking measurements of, 26–27
Trees, gnawed, nibbled or scarred by
bears, 107, 109
rabbits, 46, 51, 53, 55, 57
rodents, 63, 73, 79, 91
ungulates, 46, 148, 151, 155
Turkey, 171

Ungulates
even-toed (Artiodactyla), 19, 21, 23, 25, 147–49
odd-toed (Perissodactyla), 147

Vole, 19, 20, 40, 59, 60, 81, 84–85, 185
Clethrionomys species, 85
Lagurus species, 85
Microtus species, 85
Phenacomys species, 85

Wapiti. *See* Elk
Weasel, 15–16, 95–96, 120–25
least (*Mustela nivalis*), 122–23
long-tailed (*Mustela frenata*), 124–25, 190
short-tailed (*Mustela erminea*), 20, 120–21, 190
Weasel family. *See* Mustelid family
Wolf, 93, 94, 100–101, 102
gray (*Canis lupus*), 100–101
Wolverine (*Gulo gulo*), 24, 93, 95, 96, 130–31
Woodchuck (*Marmota monax*), 66–67
Woodrat (*Neotoma*), 59, 82–83, 89

184

How many of these sample tracks can you identify from field photographs?

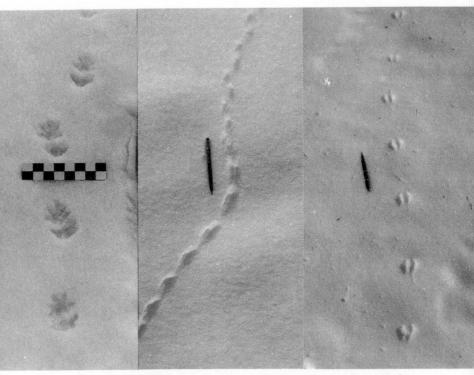

Left: Opossum tracks in the alternating walking pattern with a 1-inch grid marker; note the "thumb" on the hind foot track. PHOTOGRAPH COURTESY OF HARRY HARTWELL. *Center: A shrew trail next to a 5.5-inch pencil. The shrew makes a two-print (merged four-print) hopping pattern in the lower left, then slows to a walking, alternating pattern as it moves toward the top. Right: Vole tracks heading up the photo in the typical vole two-print track pattern. Note the long intergroup distances compared to the mouse or shrew tracks in other photos. (Pencil is 5.5 inches long.)*

Snowshoe hare tracks (larger) leading right and mouse tracks crossing left. Note that the mouse's front feet are side by side and that its intergroup distances are small. (Pencil is 5.5 inches long.)

Left: Jackrabbit tracks in the four-print hopping pattern heading away from the camera, the larger hind feet ahead of front feet. (Pencil is 5.5 inches long.) Below: Gray squirrel tracks heading up the photo with the front feet paired side by side. PHOTOGRAPH COURTESY OF WILLIAM RICHARDSON.

Red squirrel tracks heading back and forth next to a moose trail. The squirrel tracks are in a two-print (merged four-print) pattern and feet are dragging—a very common track pattern in soft snow.

Ground squirrel tracks heading in both directions; the one by the pencil (5.5 inches) is heading up the photo. Notice its diagonally placed front feet.

Prairie dog tracks heading away from the camera. At first the prairie dog is hopping in a four-print pattern; then it slows to walk in an alternating pattern. A burrow lies to the center top amidst the trampled feeding area. (Pencil is 5.5 inches long.)

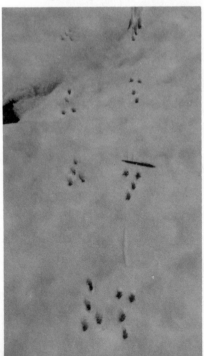

A beaver trail (left) next to a mink trail (right). The beaver's tail is dragging and covering up most of its prints, although the hind-foot prints are still obvious in some spots. The mink is loping in mustelid two-print fashion.

This porcupine is walking toward the camera in its typical pigeon-toed alternating track pattern. (Pencil is 5.5 inches long.)

Two coyote trails. The coyote on the left walked in the alternating track pattern; the one on the right galloped, making a "C-shaped" rotatory gallop, although it is difficult to separate the four-print groups. Note how their feet drag.

Right: *A close-up of coyote tracks in a trotting two-print pattern heading up the photo. The pads and claws on the front toes are visible. (Pencil is 5.5 inches long.)*
Below: *Two swift fox trails. The fox on the left walked in an alternating track pattern, its prints nearly in a straight line. The one on the right galloped in a common four-print galloping pattern. (Pencil is 5.5 inches long.)*

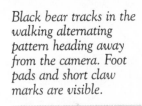

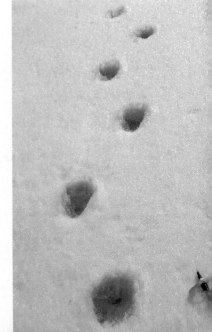

Black bear tracks in the walking alternating pattern heading away from the camera. Foot pads and short claw marks are visible.

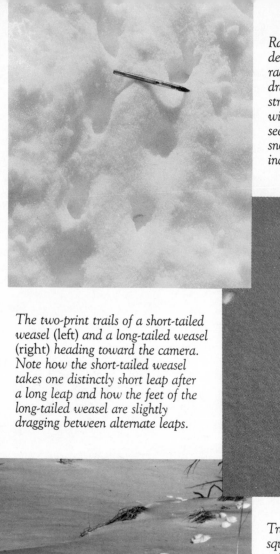

Raccoon tracks in deep snow. The raccoon's body is dragging, and its straddle is much wider than you would see in light or firm snow. (Pencil is 5.5 inches long.)

The two-print trails of a short-tailed weasel (left) and a long-tailed weasel (right) heading toward the camera. Note how the short-tailed weasel takes one distinctly short leap after a long leap and how the feet of the long-tailed weasel are slightly dragging between alternate leaps.

Tracks of a red squirrel hopping in a four-print pattern (left) and a marten loping in a two-print pattern (right), both heading away from the camera. You can just see the toe pads of the marten, but this is uncommon in soft, deep snow. (Pencil is 5.5 inches long.)

Right: *The loping four-print track pattern of a striped skunk. The four-print groups are spaced closely together. (Pencil is 5.5 inches long.)*
Below: *A typical river otter trail, tail flopping and feet making a three-print pattern. The other trails are coyotes walking.*

A lynx trail as it leads away from the camera in an alternating track pattern. Tracks are neat and round and show no foot drags.
PHOTOGRAPH COURTESY OF ROBERT STEPHENSON.

Tracks of a deer walking toward the camera in an alternating track pattern. Note how the feet drag and make slide marks as they step into the snow. The slot made by the leg (at the pencil) is narrow and a clue for distinguishing between ungulates. (Pencil is 5.5 inches long.)

Right: The trail of a moose walking towards the camera in an alternating track pattern. Its feet are dragging, leaving marks that have two grooves made by its toes. Below: The walking tracks of a bighorn sheep. The smaller hind foot has overstepped the larger, more splayed, front foot. (Pencil is 5.5 inches long.)